European Institute for
Crime Prevention and Control,
affiliated with the United Nations
P.O. BOX 34
FIN-00931 Helsinki, Finland

Publication Series No. 28

CRIME PREVENTION STRATEGIES IN EUROPE AND NORTH AMERICA

John Graham
Trevor Bennett

February 1995

Copies can be purchased from:

Academic Bookstore   Criminal Justice Press
P.O. Box 128   P.O. Box 249
FIN-00100 Helsinki   Monsey, New York 10952
Finland   USA

ISBN 951 53 0178 5 ✓
ISSN 1237 4741

TABLE OF CONTENTS

PREFACE TO THE SECOND EDITION AND ACKNOWLEDGEMENTS

This book comprises one of the most comprehensive accounts of crime prevention strategies in print. It provides a detailed description of a wide range of crime prevention strategies adopted throughout Europe and North America and offers policy makers and practitioners worldwide a step-by-step guide to preventing crime in their own country. It considerably expands upon the first edition published in 1990, which quickly became out of print, and includes more than twenty new crime prevention initiatives (see Appendix 1 for a full list of all projects). It updates the findings of research and evaluation in the field of crime prevention and provides additional information in a number of areas, from bullying in schools to the design of strategies to prevent revictimisation.

Whilst much of the material presented in the first edition is retained, the current edition represents a complete re-working and updating of this material. The second edition has benefited from recent developments in the way in which crime prevention is defined and conceptualised and in the introduction, these new developments are reflected in a more informed discussion of how to define and classify crime prevention. New material is also presented here on different organisational structures for developing policy at the national level.

Chapter 1 is now titled criminality prevention as opposed to social crime prevention and new material is presented on the role of families and schools in preventing criminality and how they might work more closely with each other to improve their capacity to socialise young people. Chapter 2 has been reorganised to take account of the recent work of Ron Clarke in refining a framework for classifying situational crime prevention. This chapter also contains new material on displacement and reports the first findings from the British Safer Cities programme. Chapter 3 benefits from a much clearer breakdown of approaches to community-based crime prevention and Chapter 4 now contains a detailed guide on how to evaluate crime prevention initiatives.

This second edition has been prepared by Mr John Graham of the Research and Planning Unit of the Home Office in England and Wales and Dr Trevor Bennett of the Institute of Criminology, University of Cambridge. They would like to thank Dr Matti Joutsen of HEUNI for offering his support and encouragement during the preparation of this book and members of the Home Office for providing valuable advice and comments on earlier drafts.

John Graham
Trevor Bennett

London, 8 February 1995

SUMMARY

This book provides a detailed account of a wide range of crime prevention strategies and measures in Europe and North America and offers advice and guidance to policy makers and practitioners on those most likely to be effective and how the process of preventing crime can be methodically planned, implemented and evaluated.

In the Introduction, issues related to defining and classifying crime prevention are discussed within an overall context of competing explanations for the substantial rise in crime in western societies in the last thirty years and the simultaneous expansion of a wide range of administrative arrangements and strategies for preventing and reducing crime. Three main categories of crime prevention are identified - criminality prevention, situational crime prevention and community crime prevention - and the parameters delineating which crimes are included in the study and how wide the concept of prevention should be applied are set out. Essentially, the book focuses on the prevention of property crimes, such as burglary, robbery and theft (including shoplifting) and 'street' crimes, such as assault, criminal damage and auto-crime and the concept of prevention is taken to exclude those activities performed by agencies of the criminal justice system.

Chapter 1 covers the prevention of criminality, which is concerned with reducing the dispositions of individuals to commit offences. This involves the manipulation of the principal socio-economic structures and institutions of society which influence the personal and social development of children, young people and their families. To this end, six areas of social policy are identified as most relevant - urban, health, family, education, youth and employment. Of these, the last four form the main focus of this chapter.

Family policy

Research has shown that the structure and functioning of families play a crucial role in promoting effective socialisation and social integration and thus in inhibiting or preventing delinquency. Where children are neglected or inconsistently disciplined by their parents or where they experience disrupted and disruptive family lives, they are at risk of committing offences as they enter young adulthood, particularly if one or more of their parents themselves have been involved in offending. Where families experience severe deprivation, isolation and poverty, the risks are compounded.

Seven forms of family intervention are identified as likely to assist in reducing or preventing the development of criminal propensities by enhancing the capacity of families to offer protection, supervision, discipline and care: (i) preventing teenage pregnancies; (ii) providing support and advisory services for mothers during pregnancy and infancy; (iii) providing guidance for improving the quality of parenting; (iv) providing pre-school education for children living in deprived families or experiencing specific difficulties; (v) offering support to parents at specific times of stress; (vi) developing strategies for preventing child abuse and keeping families intact; and (vii) preventing youth homelessness.

Education policy

Like families, schools play a major part in the personal and social development of children and young people. Research has shown that through their capacity to motivate, educate and integrate pupils, schools can influence the behaviour of young people and ultimately whether or not they may become offenders. The three mechanisms through which they are most likely to achieve these aims are by maximising their educational performance, ensuring their regular attendance at school and preventing them from behaving disruptively in school. All three 'outcomes' are in turn influenced by the organisation and 'ethos' of schools and the principal components of what makes an effective school and how schools can change for the better are outlined in detail. Programmes for preventing bullying, truancy and disruptive behaviour in school are assessed and ways in which schools can prevent criminality by enhancing their links with families are also suggested.

Youth policy

In western societies which increasingly foster high material expectations whilst, for many young people, withholding the means to acquire them, leisure and cultural activities are becoming increasingly important sources of identity, status and independence. This section describes a number of highly imaginative projects which provide activities for young people ranging from sport and music to theatre and dance, and which involve young people themselves in developing and running such projects. Although there is little research evidence to show that youth work in general or youth clubs in particular can reduce or prevent criminality, youth workers can provide educational, supervisory and leisure and informational services which may help to prevent some young people from becoming offenders and detached or outreach work is singled out as the most important aspect of youth work in preventing criminality. By contacting and developing relationships with groups of the most marginalised young people and mediating between them and networks of local agencies, detached youth workers can provide young people with access to a range of resources at the local level and integrate them into the community.

Five main strategies are identified by which youth workers can contribute to the prevention of criminality: (i) to identify peer group networks and patterns of behaviour which lead to conflicts and offending; (ii) to explore the relationships between these patterns and situations and the individual and collective needs and identities of the young people concerned; (iii) to seek to encourage alternative sources of acquiring self-esteem, prestige and status; (iv) to facilitate access to the services of local agencies; and (v) to supervise young people on the streets and seek to divert them from crime-prone situations into legitimate, self-chosen activities.

Employment policy

Despite the equivocal findings of research on the relationship between unemployment and crime, it is accepted that unemployment and crime, at least in individual cases, may reinforce each other. Providing high quality training and work experience, securing a wide range of employment opportunities and encouraging the development of formal and informal employment networks are the three main forms of employment programme discussed in this section. At least five elements of employment programmes are identified as potentially influencing offending dispositions: (i) job satisfaction and positive feedback on performance; (ii) opportunities for promotion and advancement; (iii) rapport with supervisors and co-workers; (iv) opportunities to use one's skills and learn new skills; and (v) the provision of status and incremental rewards.

Chapter 2 presents an overview of situational crime prevention, which comprises measures aimed at reducing opportunities for committing offences. Its focus is on offences rather than offenders and its attraction lies in its capacity to provide practical, often simple and relatively inexpensive solutions in a wide variety of locations and situations. Three main kinds of measures are discussed: those which increase the effort of offending, those which increase the risks of offending and those which reduce the rewards of offending. These are followed by examples of crime prevention initiatives which combine a number of situational measures and a discussion on the issue of displacement, which is potentially a serious threat to the efficacy of situational measures.

Increasing the effort of offending

Four methods which increase the effort of offending are identified: (i) target hardening, which increases the strength of physical barriers to targets by installing or improving security devices such as locks and safes; (ii) access control, which comprises restricting access to specific areas in which targets may be located (e.g. apartment blocks, housing estates or shopping centres) by installing, for example, entry phones or automatic ticket machines; (iii) deflecting offenders, which consists of diverting offenders away from potential targets and towards more acceptable ones by, for example, introducing traffic flow restrictions which keep 'outsiders' away from specific residential or commercial areas; and (iv) controlling facilitators, which means ensuring that the means for committing certain offences are made unavailable by, for example, screening airline passengers for weapons or proscribing the ownership of firearms.

Increasing the risks of offending

The real or perceived threat of detection, apprehension and/or conviction can be increased by introducing, or increasing the level of formal, informal and natural surveillance. Formal surveillance is exercised by people who are specifically employed for that purpose, such as the police and security personnel. Informal surveillance is conducted by people employed for other purposes but who, as part of their job, also carry out surveillance duties, such as the caretakers of residential premises or schools. In both of these cases, the capacity to exercise effective surveillance can be enhanced through installing closed circuit television (CCTV) and/or alarms. Natural surveillance comprises manipulating the physical environment in such a way that the capacity of ordinary citizens to exercise a degree of surveillance as they go about their everyday activities is increased. Natural surveillance can be enhanced by, for example, carefully designing the structure and layout of residential areas and housing estates, by mixing land uses in urban areas or by providing better street lighting.

Reducing the rewards of offending

Reducing the expected benefits from committing offences can be achieved by physically removing potential targets of crime, such as large amounts of cash; by marking property so that it is more easily identifiable and therefore less marketable and of less value; by removing inducements or temptations to commit offences by, for example, repairing broken windows or removing partially damaged cars quickly; and by setting rules which restrict and control the behaviour of employees and citizens who might otherwise be tempted to bend the rules in their favour by, for example, tightening up stock control procedures.

Displacement

It could be argued that criminal activity targeted by situational measures can be displaced to other targets, locations, times or offences or to being committed by different methods or even different offenders. Most evaluations of crime prevention initiatives do not adequately measure displacement effects, but those which do suggest that not all crime is displaced.

Chapter 3 describes programmes which draw on both situational measures and measures to prevent criminality and locates them within a community-based framework of action. They involve encouraging members of the community in organising a collective rather than an individual response to crime. Three distinctive approaches to community crime prevention are presented: (i) community organisation; (ii) community defence and (iii) community development. These are followed by a discussion on the role of the police in community crime prevention initiatives.

Community organisation

Based on the premise that rapid social change weakens the social organisation and identity of communities and subsequently their capacity to socialise and control their young people, the community organisation approach aims to mobilise neighbourhood resources to prevent crime and criminality. Overall, there is little evidence to suggest that attempts to reduce crime and criminality through community organising have been successful, particularly in disadvantaged communities with high crime rates.

Community defence

The community defence model arose out of a growing fear of crime and disorder in urban areas and the resultant desire for greater self protection, particularly from outside predators. Measures to reduce social and physical disorder, such as reducing loitering and speeding up the repair of buildings, are combined with increasing foot patrols by the police and local citizens. To date there is little evidence on whether citizen patrols may be effective in reducing fear of crime or crime rates.

An additional feature of this approach is neighbourhood watch, which consists of encouraging citizens to watch out for and report suspicious incidents in their neighbourhood to the police. Some neighbourhood watch schemes meet formally to exchange information about local problems of crime and disorder and work together to devise ways of tackling them. Participation in neighbourhood watch schemes diminishes in proportion to the degree of social disadvantage, resident turnover and social fragmentation. There is no conclusive evidence that neighbourhood watch reduces crime and in some cases it may lead to increases in fear of crime.

Community development

Community development arises in response to urban disintegration. It involves the rebuilding of the social, economic and physical fabric of communities and can be divided into four strategies (although programmes invariably draw on more than one of these): (i) improvements to the built environment; (ii) the decentralisation of housing estate management and services programmes; (iii) improving housing allocation policies; and (iv) social and economic regeneration. Improvements to the built environment comprise design, maintenance and repair programmes and building and investment programmes. These improvements have been found to reduce crime, along with the decentralisation of housing estate management and other services to individual estates and the avoidance of housing allocation procedures which concentrate the poor and most disadvantaged in the same areas, or raise child densities beyond a certain threshold. Programmes which combine physical, environmental and social improvements with economic regeneration at the grass roots level are most likely to produce long term improvements in community crime rates.

The role of the police

Two forms of policing are often components of community-based strategies to prevent crime: (i) community policing; and (ii) problem-oriented policing. The former is concerned with improving the accessibility and visibility of the police by consulting, collaborating with, and obtaining the consent of, local residents. Sector and team policing have been introduced at the area level and community constables and police shops at the local level. Overall, the concept of community policing still needs to be refined and the process of implementation improved before it is likely to have a significant impact on crime rates. The latter is concerned with adapting the problem-solving process to the policing of community issues. It is more likely to reduce crime at the local as opposed to the area level.

Chapter 4 covers the planning, implementation and evaluation of crime prevention at the local level. A five-stage sequence of events characterises the crime prevention process: (i) obtaining data on the crime problem; (ii) analysing and interpreting the data; (iii) devising preventive strategies; (iv) implementation; and (v) evaluation.

Obtaining information

Data need to be collected on a wide range of factors, including information on the area and its buildings, the location and nature of incidents and the 'actors' involved. Various sources of information can be used in addition to police crime data, such as offender and victim surveys and observation. The limitations of police data need to be recognised, as does the importance of collecting information on repeat victimisation. Special training in the basic techniques of data collection should be promoted and where possible the importance of information gathering should be emphasised.

Data analysis and interpretation

Once collected, patterns in the data need to be identified, interpreted and explained. Plotting trends and constructing maps can be useful here. As part of the process of interpretation, information and patterns observed in relation to crime need to be combined with information and patterns observed in relation to physical, social and demographic data.

Devising strategies

Once crime patterns have been established and interpreted, strategies need to be devised which encompass interventions aimed at different incidents or targets, at different levels (individuals, groups, neighbourhoods) and by different agencies. It is important to know through what 'causal mechanisms' specific interventions might work and to set priorities.

Implementation

If possible, the process of devising preventive strategies should also include the anticipation of any constraints which might affect the successful implementation of the programme. A number of single- and multi-agency strategies exist for implementing crime prevention initiatives, but from experience it is known that various obstacles can undermine the success of even the best laid plans. The obstacles to effective multi-agency implementation include: (i) failure to coordinate action; (ii) conflicting priorities; (iii) conflicting professional perceptions of the problem and how to respond to it; (iv) threats to an agency's professional autonomy and area of responsibility; and (v) lack of knowledge about each other's roles and responsibilities. A number of procedures for overcoming some of these difficulties are presented, such as ensuring that any structures for delivering crime prevention initiatives are flexible and have the full backing of the local community, clearly identifying which agency should take the lead role, and employing professional coordinators to manage the programme.

Evaluation

The final stage in the crime prevention process is to evaluate the programme. To date, this has probably been the most neglected aspect of the crime prevention process and is arguably the most difficult to accomplish with any degree of quality. Evaluations tend to be time-consuming, costly and sometimes threatening, but are essential if knowledge about what works under what circumstances is to be accumulated. Evaluations fall into two distinctive but related parts - process and outcome. The former is concerned with monitoring implementation and the latter with determining the impact of the programme on crime and other outcomes. The nature, strengths and weaknesses of the two most scientifically rigorous outcome evaluation designs are described in detail - experiments and quasi experiments.

RESUME (French Summary)

Cet ouvrage fournit une description détaillée d'une grande diversité de stratégies et de mesures pour la lutte contre la délinquance en Europe et en Amérique du Nord. Il offre des conseils et des lignes directrices aux preneurs de décision et aux praticiens sur celles qui seront probablement les plus efficaces et sur la façon dont le processus de lutte contre la délinquance peut être planifié, mis en oeuvre et évalué de manière méthodique.

Dans l'Introduction, sont abordées les questions se rapportant à la définition et à la classification de la lutte contre la délinquance dans le cadre des explications rivales de l'importante augmentation de la criminalité dans les sociétés occidentales, au cours des trente dernières années, accompagnée simultanément de l'accroissement d'une grande variété de dispositions administratives et de stratégies pour lutter contre la délinquance et la réduire. Trois catégories principales de lutte contre la délinquance y sont identifiées : la lutte contre la criminalité, la lutte situationnelle contre la délinquance et la lutte communautaire contre la délinquance. Les paramètres délimitant les délits qui sont inclus dans l'étude et l'envergure à donner au concept de lutte y sont expliqués. L'ouvrage se concentre principalement sur la lutte contre la délinquance contre les biens, tels que les cambriolages, les vols qualifiés et les vols (dont le vol à l'étalage) et les délits 'de la rue', tels que les agressions, les dégradations criminelles et les vols automobiles, et on accepte que le concept de la lutte exclut les activités entreprises par les agences du système de la justice criminelle.

Le chapitre 1 couvre la lutte contre la criminalité, qui s'intéresse à la réduction des inclinations d'un individu à commettre des crimes et des délits. Cela exige la manipulation des structures et institutions socio-économiques principales de la société, qui ont une influence sur le développement personnel et social des enfants, des jeunes et de leur famille. A cette fin, on a identifié six domaines de politique sociale s'y rapportant : politique urbaine, la santé, la famille, l'éducation, la jeunesse et l'emploi. Parmi ceux-ci, le chapitre se concentre particulièrement sur les quatre derniers.

La politique de la famille

La recherche montre que la structure et la façon dont fonctionnent les familles jouent un rôle fondamental dans la promotion d'une socialisation efficace et de l'intégration sociale, permettant ainsi d'inhiber ou d'empêcher la délinquance. Lorsque les enfants sont délaissés ou ne sont pas disciplinés de façon régulière et logique par leurs parents, ou bien lorsque leur vie de famille est perturbée et perturbatrice, ils courent le risque de commettre des crimes et délits lorsqu'ils deviennent de jeunes adultes, particulièrement si l'un des parents ou plus sont eux mêmes des délinquants. Lorsque les familles sont sérieusement dépossédées, isolées et pauvres, les risques sont encore plus grands.

Sept formes d'intervention sur les familles sont identifiées comme permettant probablement la réduction ou la prévention du développement des propensions criminelles en mettant en valeur la capacité des familles à offrir la protection, la surveillance, la discipline et la garde : (i) empêcher les grossesses chez les adolescentes, (ii) apporter un soutien et des conseils aux mères pendant la grossesse et la petite enfance ; (iii) fournir des conseils pour améliorer la qualité des méthodes parentales, (iv) fournir une éducation pré-scolaire pour les enfants qui vivent dans des familles dépossédées ou qui font face à des difficultés spécifiques, (v) offrir un soutien aux parents à des périodes spécifiques de tension, (vi) développer des stratégies pour empêcher les mauvais traitements infligés aux enfants et conserver les familles intactes, et (vii) empêcher que les jeunes se retrouvent sans abris.

La politique de l'éducation

Tout comme les familles, les écoles jouent un rôle majeur dans le développement personnel et social des enfants et des jeunes. La recherche montre que grâce à leur capacité à motiver, éduquer et intégrer les élèves, les écoles peuvent avoir une influence sur le comportement des jeunes et sur la possibilité qu'ils deviennent ou pas des délinquants. Les trois mécanismes grâce auxquels il est probable qu'elles puissent parvenir à ces objectifs sont de maximiser leurs performances pédagogiques, de s'assurer de leur présence régulière à l'école et de les empêcher de se comporter de façon perturbatrice à l'école. Ces trois 'résultats' sont également influencés par l'organisation et 'l'esprit' de l'école. Les composantes principales permettant à une école d'être efficace et de se perfectionner sont décrites en détail. Les programmes de lutte contre les brimades, l'absentéisme et les comportements perturbateurs à l'école sont évalués et sont également proposées des méthodes grâce auxquelles les écoles peuvent empêcher la criminalité en mettant en valeur leurs liens avec les familles.

La politique de la jeunesse

Dans les sociétés occidentales qui encouragent de plus en plus de grandes attentes matérielles alors que pour de nombreux jeunes, elles sont inaccessibles, les activités culturelles et de loisirs deviennent de plus en plus la source d'identité, de statut et d'indépendance. Cette section décrit plusieurs projets hautement imaginatifs qui offrent aux jeunes des activités allant du sport et de la musique au théâtre et à la danse, les jeunes participant au développement et à la direction à donner à ces projets. Bien qu'il existe peu de preuves découlant de recherches pour démontrer que le travail avec les jeunes en général ou que les foyers de jeunes en particulier peuvent réduire ou empêcher la criminalité, les éducateurs peuvent fournir des services pédagogiques, de surveillance, de loisirs et d'information qui peuvent empêcher certains jeunes de devenir des délinquants et les travaux des éducateurs ou des assistants sociaux sont identifiés comme étant l'aspect le plus important du travail avec les jeunes, dans la lutte contre la criminalité. En contactant et en développant des relations avec des groupes des jeunes les plus marginaux et en jouant le rôle de médiateurs entre eux et les agences locales, les éducateurs peuvent permettre aux jeunes d'accéder à une gamme de ressources au niveau local et de s'intégrer dans la communauté.

Cinq stratégies principales sont identifiées auxquelles peuvent contribuer les animateurs de jeunesse pour lutter contre la criminalité : (i) identifier les réseaux des pairs et les modèles de comportement qui mènent à des conflits et à la délinquance, (ii) explorer les relations entre ces modèles et situations et les besoins individuels et collectifs ainsi que l'identité des jeunes concernés, (iii) chercher à encourager d'autres sources pour acquérir le respect de soi, le prestige et le statut, (iv) faciliter l'accès aux services des agences locales et (v) surveiller les jeunes dans la rue et chercher à les écarter de situations prédisposant à la délinquance, pour les diriger vers des activités légitimes et qu'ils choisissent eux-mêmes.

La politique de l'emploi

Malgré les résultats équivoques de la recherche sur la relation entre le chômage et la délinquance, il est accepté que le chômage et la délinquance, du moins dans des cas individuels, peuvent se renforcer l'un et l'autre. L'apport d'un apprentissage de haute qualité et de stages en entreprise, l'offre d'une grande gamme de possibilités d'emploi et l'encouragement à développer des réseaux d'emploi formels et informels sont les trois formes principales du programme de l'emploi abordé dans cette section. Au moins cinq éléments de programmes d'emploi sont identifiés comme ayant un potentiel d'influence sur la propension à la délinquance : (i) la satisfaction de l'emploi et la réponse positive aux performances, (ii) les opportunités de promotion et d'avancement, (iii) le rapport avec les chefs et les collègues, (iv) les occasions d'utiliser ses compétences et d'en apprendre de nouvelles et (v) la présence d'un statut et de primes croissantes.

Le chapitre 2 présente une étude de la lutte situationnelle contre la délinquance, qui comprend des mesures destinées à réduire les opportunités de commettre des délits. Il se concentre sur les délits plutôt que sur les délinquants et son attrait réside dans sa capacité à fournir des solutions pratiques, souvent simples et relativement peu coûteuses dans une grande variété de lieux et de situations. Trois sortes principales de mesures y sont abordées : celles qui accroissent les efforts à faire pour devenir un délinquant, celles qui accroissent les risques de délinquance et celles qui réduisent les récompenses de la délinquance. Suivent des exemples d'initiatives dans la lutte contre la délinquance, qui associent un nombre de mesures situationnelles et une discussion sur la question du transfert, qui constitue une menace potentielle sérieuse pour l'efficacité des mesures situationnelles.

L'accroissement des efforts pour devenir un délinquant

Quatre méthodes qui accroissent les efforts à faire pour devenir un délinquant sont identifiées : (i) le durcissement des cibles, qui augmente la force des barrières physiques protégeant les cibles en installant ou en améliorant les dispositifs de sécurité tels que des verrous de sécurité et des coffres, (ii) le contrôle de l'accès, ce qui comprend la restriction de l'accès aux zones spécifiques dans lesquelles se trouvent les cibles (par ex. appartements, cités ou centres commerciaux) en installant, par exemple, des téléphones à l'entrée ou des distributeurs automatiques de tickets ; (iii) détourner les délinquants, ce qui consiste à écarter les délinquants des cibles potentielles et à les diriger vers des cibles plus acceptables, par exemple, en introduisant des restrictions de circulation qui permettent de garder les 'gens du dehors' à l'écart de zones résidentielles ou commerciales spécifiques; et (iv) des aides de contrôle, à savoir s'assurer que les moyens de commettre certains délits sont rendus inaccessibles, par exemple, en dépistant les passagers d'avion porteurs d'armes ou en interdisant la possession d'armes à feu.

L'accroissement des risques de délinquance

La menace réelle ou perçue de détection, d'arrestation et/ou de condamnation peut être accrue en introduisant ou en augmentant le niveau de surveillance formelle, informelle et naturelle. La surveillance formelle est exercée par des gens qui sont employés spécifiquement à cet effet, tels que la police ou le personnel de sécurité. La surveillance informelle est réalisée par des gens employés à d'autres fins mais qui, dans leur emploi, effectuent également des tâches de surveillance, tels que les concierges de locaux résidentiels ou d'écoles. Dans ces deux cas, la capacité à exercer une surveillance efficace peut être améliorée grâce à l'installation de télévision en circuit fermé (TVCF) et/ou des sirènes d'alarmes. La surveillance naturelle comprend la manipulation de l'environnement physique pour permettre aux citoyens ordinaires de mieux exercer un certain degré de surveillance pendant qu'ils effectuent leurs activités quotidiennes. Il est possible d'améliorer la surveillance naturelle grâce, par exemple, à une conception étudiée de la structure et de l'arrangement des zones résidentielles et des cités, en mélangeant l'usage des terrains en zones urbaines ou en fournissant un meilleur éclairage public.

La réduction des récompenses de la délinquance

Il est possible de réduire les avantages attendus en commettant des délits grâce au retrait physique des cibles potentielles de la délinquance, telles que les gros volumes d'argent liquide, par le marquage des biens afin qu'ils soient plus faciles à identifier et donc moins faciles à commercialiser et d'une valeur inférieure, par le retrait des incitations ou tentations à commettre des délits, par exemple, en réparant rapidement les fenêtres cassées ou en retirant rapidement les véhicules partiellement endommagés et enfin par l'entrée en vigueur de règlements qui restreignent et contrôlent le comportement des employés et des citoyens qui autrement, pourraient être tentés d'infléchir les règlements à leur avantage par exemple, en introduisant des procédures plus strictes de contrôle des stocks.

Le transfert

On peut avancer que l'activité criminelle ciblée par les mesures situationnelles peut être transférée à d'autres cibles, lieux, heures ou délits ou bien être commise par d'autres méthodes ou même par d'autres délinquants. La plupart des évaluations des initiatives de lutte contre la délinquance ne mesure pas de façon adéquate les effets du transfert, mais celles qui en donnent une mesure suggèrent que ce ne sont pas tous les délits qui sont transférés.

Le chapitre 3 décrit les programmes qui s'appuient à la fois sur les mesures situationnelles et sur les mesures destinées à lutter contre la criminalité et les place dans un cadre d'action s'appuyant sur la communauté. Ils consistent à encourager les membres de la communauté à organiser une réponse collective plutôt qu'individuelle à la délinquance. Trois approches distinctes de la lutte communautaire contre la délinquance y sont présentées : (i) l'organisation communautaire, (ii) la défense communautaire et (iii) le développement communautaire. Elles sont suivies d'une discussion sur le rôle de la police dans les initiatives communautaires de lutte contre la délinquance.

L'organisation communautaire

En partant de l'hypothèse que le changement social rapide affaiblit l'organisation sociale et l'identité des communautés et par conséquent, leur capacité à se fréquenter et à contrôler ses jeunes, l'approche de l'organisation communautaire a pour but de mobiliser les ressources d'un quartier pour empêcher la délinquance et la criminalité. Dans l'ensemble, il existe peu de preuves suggérant que les tentatives de réduction de la délinquance et de la criminalité au travers d'une organisation communautaire ont réussi, particulièrement dans les communautés défavorisées, aux taux élevés de délinquance.

La défense communautaire

Le modèle de la défense communautaire a émané d'une peur croissante de la délinquance et des troubles dans les zones urbaines et le désir résultant de se protéger davantage, particulièrement contre les prédateurs venant de l'extérieur. Les mesures pour réduire les troubles sociaux et physiques, telles que la réduction du nombre de flâneurs suspects et l'accélération de la réparation des bâtiments, s'associent au nombre plus grand de rondes à pied par la police et les résidents. Jusqu'à présent, il existe peu de preuves indiquant si les rondes de résidents peuvent être efficaces dans la réduction de la peur de la délinquance ou des taux de délinquance.

Une caractéristique supplémentaire de cette approche est la surveillance par les résidents, qui consiste à encourager les particuliers à ouvrir l'oeil et à informer la police d'incidents suspects dans leur quartier. Certains de ces programmes de surveillance par les résidents organisent des réunions formelles pour échanger des informations sur les problèmes locaux de délinquance et de troubles et collaborent afin de concevoir des méthodes pour les solutionner. La participation aux programmes de surveillance par les résidents diminue proportionnellement au degré de désavantage social, de mouvement des résidents et de fragmentation sociale. Il n'existe aucune preuve concluante que la surveillance par les résidents réduit la délinquance et dans certains cas, elle peut entraîner une augmentation de la peur de la délinquance.

Le développement communautaire

Le développement communautaire découle de la réponse à la désintégration urbaine. Il fait appel à la reconstruction du tissu social, économique et physique des communautés et peut être divisé en quatre stratégies (bien que les programmes s'appuient invariablement sur plusieurs de ces stratégies) : (i) des améliorations apportées à l'agglomération, (ii) la décentralisation de la gestion des cités et des programmes de services, (iii) l'amélioration de la politique d'attribution des logements et (iv) la régénération sociale et économique. Les améliorations apportées à l'agglomération comprennent les programmes de conception, d'entretien et de réparation et des programmes de construction et d'investissement. On a découvert que ces améliorations réduisent la délinquance, ainsi que la décentralisation de la gestion des cités et d'autres services vers des cités individuelles, tout comme l'élimination des procédures d'attribution des logements qui entraînent la concentration des pauvres et des plus défavorisés dans les mêmes zones ou accroissent les densités infantiles au delà d'un certain seuil. Les programmes qui associent les améliorations physiques, sociales et de l'environnement à une régénération économique à la base ont davantage de chances de produire des améliorations à long terme des taux de délinquance communautaire.

Le rôle de la police

Deux formes du maintien de l'ordre font souvent partie des stratégies de lutte contre la délinquance s'appuyant sur la communauté : (i) le maintien de l'ordre communautaire et (ii) le maintien de l'ordre s'orientant sur des problèmes. Le premier s'intéresse à l'amélioration de l'accessibilité et de la visibilité de la police en consultant, en collaborant avec et en obtenant l'assentiment des résidents du quartier. Le maintien de l'ordre d'un secteur par équipe a été introduit au niveau des zones et les policiers communautaires et les ateliers de police au niveau du quartier. Dans l'ensemble, le concept du maintien de l'ordre communautaire doit encore être raffiné et le processus de mise en oeuvre amélioré avant de pouvoir avoir un impact significatif sur les taux de délinquance. Le deuxième s'intéresse à adapter le processus de résolution des problèmes au maintien de l'ordre dans les problèmes communautaires. Il a davantage de chances de réduire la délinquance au niveau du quartier plutôt qu'au niveau de la zone.

Le chapitre 4 recouvre la planification, la mise en oeuvre et l'évaluation de la lutte contre la délinquance au niveau du quartier. Une série d'événements en cinq étapes caractérise le processus de prévention de la délinquance : (i) l'obtention de données concernant le problème de la délinquance, (ii) l'analyse et l'interprétation des données, (iii) la création de stratégies préventives, (iv) la mise en oeuvre et (v) l'évaluation.

L'obtention de l'information

Il faut recueillir des données sur un grand éventail de facteurs, dont les informations sur la zone et ses bâtiments, le lieu et la nature des incidents et les 'acteurs' y participant. On peut utiliser diverses sources d'information en plus des données de délinquance de la police, telles que les études réalisées auprès des délinquants et des victimes et l'observation. Il faut reconnaître les limites des données de la police, ainsi que l'importance de recueillir des informations sur les représailles répétées. Il faut promouvoir une formation spéciale dans les techniques de base de recueil de données et dans la mesure du possible, il faut mettre en valeur l'importance du recueil des informations.

L'analyse des données et l'interprétation

Une fois que les données sont recueillies, il faut identifier les modèles suivis par les données, les interpréter et les expliquer. Il peut être utile ici de créer des courbes des tendances et des cartes. Pendant le processus d'interprétation, il faut associer les informations et les modèles observés en rapport avec la délinquance aux informations et modèles observés en rapport aux données physiques, sociales et démographiques.

La conception de stratégies

Une fois que les modèles de délinquance ont été établis et interprétés, il faut concevoir des stratégies englobant des interventions sur des incidents ou cibles différents, à des niveaux différents (particuliers, groupes, quartiers) et par différents organismes. Il est important de savoir quels 'mécanismes causaux' permettront à des interventions spécifiques de fonctionner et d'établir des priorités.

La mise en oeuvre

Dans la mesure du possible, le processus de conception de stratégies préventives doit également comprendre l'anticipation de toute contrainte éventuelle qui pourrait avoir un effet sur la réussite de la mise en oeuvre du programme. Il existe un certain nombre de stratégies pour organisme unique ou plusieurs organismes dans la mise en oeuvre des initiatives de lutte contre la délinquance, mais l'expérience montre que divers obstacles peuvent menacer même les plans les mieux élaborés d'aboutir. Les obstacles à la mise en oeuvre efficace par plusieurs organismes comprennent : (i) l'échec de la coordination des actions, (ii) des priorités contradictoires, (iii) des perceptions profession-nelles contradictoires du problème et de la façon d'y répondre, (iv) la menace pour l'autonomie professionnelle d'un organisme et son domaine de respons-abilités et (v) le manque de connaissance des rôles et responsabilités de chacun. Plusieurs procédures sont présentées permettant de résoudre certaines de ces difficultés, comme de veiller à ce que toute structure pour la mise en application d'initiatives de lutte contre la délinquance est souple et est entièrement soutenue par la communauté locale, identifiant clairement l'organisme qui dirigera les mesures et employant des coordinateurs profes-sionnels afin de gérer le programme.

L'évaluation

L'étape finale du processus de lutte contre la délinquance est l'évaluation du programme. Jusqu'à présent, il a s'agit de l'aspect le plus négligé du processus de lutte contre la délinquance et est probablement le plus difficile à réaliser avec un degré quelconque de qualité. Les évaluations ont tendance à prendre beaucoup de temps, à être coûteuses et parfois menaçantes, mais elles sont essentielles si on veut pouvoir accumuler les connaissances sur ce qui réussit et dans quelles circonstances. Les évaluations sont séparées en deux parties distinctes mais en rapport l'une avec l'autre : le processus et le résultat. Le premier s'intéresse au contrôle de la mise en oeuvre et le dernier à la détermination de l'impact du programme sur la délinquance et autres résultats. La nature, les avantages et les inconvénients des deux conceptions les plus rigoureuses sur le plan scientifique pour l'évaluation des résultats sont décrits en détails : les expériences et les quasi-expériences.

ОБЩИЙ ОБЗОР (RUSSIAN SUMMARY)

В этой книге подробно рассматривается большое количество стратегий и мер по предотвращению преступлений в Европе и Северной Америке, и вниманию руководящих органов и сотрудников предлагаются советы и рекомендации по наиболее эффективным из мер и стратегий, а также приводится описание методического планирования, осуществления и развития мер по предотвращению преступлений.

Во Вступлении, в контексте различных объяснений значительного роста преступности в западных обществах за последние тридцать лет и одновременного увеличения административного вмешательства и разработки стратегий по предотвращению и уменьшению преступности, обсуждаются вопросы определения и классификации аспектов предотвращения преступлений. Определены три основные категории предотвращения преступлений - предотвращение возникновения преступности, предотвращение ситуативных преступлений и предотвращение общественных преступлений, а также параметры, определяющие тип преступлений, рассматриваемых в исследовании, вместе с широким набором концепций по предотвращению преступлений. В основном в книге уделяется внимание предотвращению преступлений против собственности, таких как хищения со взломом, грабежи и кражи (включая мелкие кражи в магазинах) и «уличные» преступления, такие как нападение, нанесение преступного ущерба и преступления, связанные с автомоб илями, при этом в концепцию предотвращения не включается деятельность уголовно-юридических органов.

В Главе 2 рассматриваются вопросы профилактики преступности, с точки зрения уменьшения наклонности отдельных лиц к совершению уголовных правонарушений. Рассматриваются принципы изменения социально-экономических структур и организаций общества, оказывающих влияние на личностное и социальное развитие детей, молодых людей и их семей. Для этого определены шесть зон социальной политики - городская зона, здравоохранение, семья, об разование, молодежь и занятость. Из этих шести четыре рассматриваются в этой главе наиболее подробно.

Семейная Политика

Исследования показывают, что структура и функции семьи играют решающую роль в эффективной социализации и социальной интеграции личности, и что таким образом снижаются и предотвращаются правонарушения. Если детям в семье не уделяется достаточного внимания, или если дисциплинарные меры в семье не проводятся достаточно последовательно, или если семейная об становка является неблагополучной, имеется риск совершения правонарушений в период, когда дети становятся молодыми людьми, в особенности если один из родителей сам совершал правонарушения. Если материальное положение семьи является чрезвычайно плохим, или если семья страдает от изоляции, этот риск значительно увеличивается. Определены семь видов семейного вмешательства, которые могут содействовать снижению или профилактике развитию криминальных наклонностей через улучшение обстановки в семье в том, что касается защиты, надзора, воспитательных мер и ухода: (i) предотвращение подростковой беременности; (ii) оказание поддержки и консультативных услуг матерям во время беременности и в раннем возрасте ребенка; (ш) советы по улучшению качества выполнения родителями их роли; (iṗ) обеспечение дошкольного образования детям из малообеспеченных семей или из семей, где ожидаются значительные трудности; (ṗ) обеспечение поддержки родителям в стрессовых ситуациях; (ṗı) разработка стратегических мер для предотвращения дурного обращения с детьми и для сохранения целостности семьи; (ṗıı) предотвращение бездомности молодых людей.

Образовательная политика

Также как и семья, школа играет значительную роль в личном и социальном развитии ребенка и молодого человека. Исследования показывают, что школы, пользуясь своими возможностями мотивировать, образовывать и интегрировать учеников, могут влиять на поведение молодых людей и на то, станут ли молодые люди правонарушителями. Имеется три основных способа достижения этих целей, максимизация образовательной функции, обеспечение регулярной посещаемости уроков и предотвращение неправильного поведения вне школы. Эти три элемента, в свою очередь, находятся под влиянием организации и «духа» школы, и в книге подробно описываются основные элементы, которые делают школу действенной организацией, а также методы улучшения школьной работы. Приводится оценка школьных программ по профилактике случаев запугивания, прогулов и неправильного поведения в школе, а также предлагаются методы профилактики преступности в школе через укрепление связи с семьей.

Принцыпы работы с молодежью

В западных обществах, где поощряются высокие материльные ожидания, но при этом зачастую молодые люди не имеют средств к осуществлению этих ожиданий, отдых и развлечения все в большей степени становятся средством самовыражения, статуса и независимости молодых людей. В данной секции описывается несколько весьма интересных проектов, обеспечивающих занятость молодых людей, от спорта и музыки до театра и танцев, при этом сами молодые люди активно участвуют в разработке и осуществлении этих проектов. Хотя и не имеется достаточных исследовательских данных, говорящих о том, что работа с молодежью вообще и клубная работа с молодежью в частности уменьшает или предотвращает правонарушения, специалисты по работе с молодежью могут оказывать услуги по образованию, надзору, обеспечению информации и проведению досуга молодых людей, что может помочь в профилактике правонарушений среди молодежи, при этом внеорганизационная работа рассматривается в качестве наиболее важного аспекта работы с молодежью в том, что касается профилактики правонарушений. Через завязывание и развитие контактов с группами наиболее маргинизированных молодых людей и оказание посреднических услуг между ними и сетью местных органов, специалисты по внеорганизационной работе с молодежью могут обеспечить молодежи доступ к целому ряду ресурсов на местном уровне и содействовать их социальной интеграции.

В секции определены пять основных стратегий, с помощью которых специалисты по работе с молодежью могут внести свою лепту в профилактику преступности: (ı) определение сети группы молодежи и элементов поведения, которые ведут к конфликтам и правонарушениям; (п) исследование взаимной связи между этими элементами и ситуациями, а также индивидуальных и коллективных потребностей и определение личностей молодых людей; (ш) поиски и обеспечение мотивации для использования других методов самовыражения, престижа и статуса; (iр) обеспечение доступа к услугам местных органов; и (р) наздор за молодыми людьми на улице и нахождение способов отвлечения их от криминогенных ситуаций и поощрение выбранной ими деятельности, если она не ведет к правонарушениям.

Политика, связанная с занятостью

Несмотря на то, что выводы исследования взаимозависимости уровня безработицы и преступности являются неоднозначными, принято считать, что безработица и правонарушения, по меньшей мере в отдельных случаях, могут быть связаны друг с другом. Обеспечение высококачественного профессионального обучения и практического опыта, предоставление широкого ряда возможностей по найму, и стимулирование развития формальных и неформальных сетей по занятости являются тремя важнейшими формами программы занятости, которая обсуждается в этой секции. Определяются по меньшей мере пять элементов, потенциально влияющих на степень предрасположенности к правонарушениям: (i) удовлетворение, получаемое от работы, и положительная мотивация в результате трудовой деятельности; (п) возможности продвижения по работе и повышения квалификации; (ш) хорошие отношения с руководителем работ и с коллегами; (iр) возможности применения трудовых навыков и обучения новым навыкам; и (р) чувство статуса и повышающееся удовлетворение, получаемое от работы.

В Главе 2 приводится обзор профилактики ситуативных преступлений, здесь рассматриваются меры, направленные на снижение возможностей для совершения правонарушений. Основнй упор делается на правонарушения, а не на правонарушителей, привлекательной чертой является способность этого подхода об еспечить практические, зачастую простые и сравнительно недорогие решения, применимые к целому ряду мест и ситуаций. Рассматриваются три основные группы мер: меры, в результате которых от правонарушителей требуются большие усилия для совершения правонарушений, меры, повышающие риск, связанный с правонарушениями, и меры, снижающие потенциалную «награду», ожидаемую в результате правонарушения. Далее следуют примеры инициатив по профилактике правонарушений, в том числе несколько ситуативных мер, а также обсуждиние вопроса о смещении фокуса усилий, что потенциально является серьезной угрозой эффективности ситуативных мер. Повышение усилий для совершения правонарушений

Определяются четыре способа повышения усилий для совершения правонарушений: (i) затруднение доступа к объекту правонарушения, куда входит усиление физически барьеров через установку или улучшение охранных приспособлений, таких как замки и сейфы; (п) контроль доступа, сюда входит ограничение доступа в те или иные зоны, где могут распологаться объекты преступлений (например, многокврартирные жилые дома, жилищные комплексы и торговые центры), через установку переговорных устройств, автоматических «б илетных» машин и т. п.; (ш) отвлечение правонарушителей в дугие зоны, что состоит, например, в направлении транспортных потоков прочь от потенциальных объектов правонарушений, расположенных в жилых или торговых комплексах в другие, менее уязвимые зоны; и (1р) контроль средств, способствующих совершению правонарушений, например, проверка авиапассажиров на предмет обнаружения оружия или запрещение владения оружием.

Повышение риска, связанного с правонарушениями

Реальная или предполагаемая угроза обнаружения, задержания и/или осуждения судом могут быть усилены через введение или повышение уровня формального, неформального и натурального надзора. Формальный надзор осуществляется людьми, специально нанятыми для этой цели, например, полицией и сотрудниками охраны. Неформальный надзор осуществляется людьми, нанятыми для выполнения других функций, которые в ходе выполнения своих служебных обязанностей также совершают обходы, например, вахтеры жилых сооружений и школ. В обоих случаях возможности выполнения эффективного надзора повышаются с установкой сети телевизионных камер (ÀÀÒÐ) и средств сигнализации. В ходе натрурального надзора принимаются меры, которые дают возможность обычным гражданам осуществлять надзор в ходе того, как они занимаются своими повседневными делами. Осуществлению натурального обзора может способствовать, например, тщательно продуманное планирование жилых комлексов, сочетание землепользователей в городских зонах и обеспечение уличного освещения.

Снижение потенциальной «награды», ожидаемой от правонарушения

Снижение потенциальной «награды» от правонарушений может быть достигнуто через физическое удаление объектов преступлений, например, больших сумм денег; через маркировку имущества таким об разом, что оно становится легко узнаваемым и в силу этого менее «продаваемым», или в силу чего снижается его продажная цена; через удаление стимулов к совершению преступления, например, через своевременную замену разбитых стекол и оперативное удаление поврежденных автомобилей; а также через введение правил и средств контроля поведения сотрудников и граждан, которые в ином случае могли бы пойти на риск и нарушить эти правила с целью извлечения выгоды, например, через усиление инвентарного контроля.

Вымещение Существует мнение, что преступная деятельность, которая подвергается ситуативным мерам, может быть вымещена и переориентирована на другие объекты, в другие места, в другое время или изменять свою форму, правонарушения могут совершаться другими способами или даже другими лицами. Большая часть оценок мер по профилактике правонарушений не обеспечивают адекватного представления о вымещении, но в тех случаях, когда оценка имеется, можно сделать вывод, что не все правонарушения вымещаются.

В Главе 3 описываются программы, сочетающие в себе как ситуативные меры, так и меры по предотвращению преступности, и эти программы рассматриваются в контексте общественной системы деятельности. Сюда входит стимулирование граждан в целях организации коллективной, в отличие от индивидуальной, реакции на преступления. Выделяются три различных подхода к общественной профилактике преступности: (1) организация общественности; (11) об щественная защита; и (111) общественное развитие. Затем следует рассмотрение роли полиции в рамках общественных инициатив профилактики преступности.

Организация общественности

Основываясь на допущении, что быстрые социальные изменения ослабляют организацию общественности и размывают общественное лицо, вследвтвие чего уменьшается способность общества социализировать и контролировать молодежь, этот подход призван мобилизовать местные общественные ресурсы в целях предотвращения преступлений и преступной деятельности. В общем и целом не имеется достаточных доказательств того, что попытки уменьшить количество преступлений через организацию общественности были успешными, в особенности в обществах, испытывающих трудности, где преступность является высокой.

Общественная защита

Эта модель возникла в результате растущего страха перед преступностью и беспорядками в городских зонах, в результате возникло желание лучше обеспечить самозащиту, в частности от налетчиков-»гастролеров». Меры по уменьшению социальных и физических аномалий, таких как снижение количества праздношатающихся и ускорение ремонта зданий, сочетаются с интенсификацией пеших патрулей силами полиции и местных граждан. В настоящее время не имеется достаточно данных в доказательство эффективности этих мер в снижении преступности и порождаемого ей страха.

Еще один элемент этого подхода - «местное наблюдение», в ходе которого граждане следят и сообщают в полицию о подозрительной активности в их районе. В рамках некоторых программ по местному наблюдению проводятся официальные встречи для обмена информацией о местных проблемах, касающихся преступности и беспорядков, и разрабатываются меры совместного решения этих проблем. Участие в схемах местного наблюдения снижается прямо пропорционально уровню превалирующих социальных сложностей в обществе, текучести местного населения и социальной разобщенности. Не имеется убедительных доказательств того, что местное наблюдение способствует снижению преступности, а в некоторых случаях оно может привести к увеличению степени страха перед возможными преступлениями.

Общественное развитие

Общественное развитие имеет место в качестве реакции на урбанальную дисинтеграцию. В ходе этого идет восстановление социальной, экономической и физической «ткани» общества, процесс может быть разделен на четыре стратегических типа (хотя программы всегда объединяют в себе элементы нескольких стратегических типов): (1) улучшение обстановки в застроенных зонах; (11) децентрализация менеджмента жилых комплексов и программ обслуживания; (111) улучшение принципов распределения жилья; и (1р) социальное и экономическое восстановление. В ходе улучшения обстановки в застроенных зонах проводятся программы по дизайну, поддержанию и ремонту, а также строительные и инвестиционные программы. Было обнаружено, что в результате этого преступность снижается вслед за децентрализацией менеджмента жилых комплексов и программ обслуживания, а также в ходе снижения количества случаев, когда зоны заселяются наиболее бедными гражданами, или когда концентрация детей в жилых комплексов превышает определенный уровень. Было обнаружено, что программы, в ходе которых сочетаются физические, местные и социальные улучшения, а также экономическое восстановление на базовом уровне, скорей всего принесут положительные долгосрочные результаты в снижении местного уровня преступности.

Роль полиции

В рамках общественной стратегии про предотвращению правонарушений полиция действует двумя способами: (i) деятельность полиции на местном уровне и (ii) деятельность полиции, направленная на решение определенных проблем. В первом случае улучшается доступность и «заметность» полиции через консультации, сотрудничество и обеспечение благоприятного общественного мнения. Секторная и групповая деятельность полиции проводится на окружном уровне, а общественные констебли и полицейские опорные пункты выполняют свои функции на местном уровне. В общем и целом концепция местной полицейской деятельности требует дальнейшего уточнения, и для достижения эффективного снижения уровня преступности процесс осуществления требует улучшения. Последнее включает в себя приспособление процесса решения проб лем к конкретным местным условиям. Более вероятным является снижение уровня преступности на местном уровне, в отличии от окружного.

В Главе 4 рассматривается планирование, внедрегие и оценка мер по предотвращению преступлений на местном уровне. Процесс профилактики преступности разбивается на пять этапов: (i) получение данных о проблемах, связанных с преступностью; (ii) анализ и интерпретация данных; (iii) создание профилактической стратегии; (iр) внедрение и (р) оценка. Получение информации

Требуется сбор данных по широкому кругу факторов, включая информацию по округу, по зданиям и сооружениям, по территориальному распределению и характеру и по участникам инцидентов. Дополнительно к данным, имеющимся у полиции, могут использоваться и другие источники информации, такие как опросы правонарушителей и жертв. Следует признать ограниченный характер данных, имеющихся у полиции, а также важность сбора информации по повторной виктимизации. Следует проводить специальные программы обучения по сбору данных, и везде, где возможно, следует подчеркивать важность сбора информации.

Анализ и интерпретация данных

После того, как данные были собраны, требуется определить, интерпретировать и объяснить характерные тенденции. В качестве составной части процесса интерпретации следует рассматривать информацию и тенденции, относящиеся к преступлениям, вместе с информацией и тенденциями, касающимися физических, социальных и демографических структур.

После того, как были определены и интерпретированы преступные тенденции, следует разарботать стратегию мер, касающихся тех или иных инцидентов и объектов на различных уровнях (индивидуальный, групповой, местных), и принимаемых различными органами. Важно занать, какой «механизм причинности» может принести наилучшие результаты, и определить приоритетность мер.

Осуществление

Если возможно, в процесс разработки превентивной стратегии следует включить ожидаемые сложности, которые могут повлиять на успешное осуществление программы. Существует несколько стратегических программ по осуществлению инициатив профилактики преступности, с участием одного или нескольких органов, но из опыта известно, что различные препятствия могут подоровать успех даже самых лучших планов. В число этих препятствий входят: (i) неумение координировать действия; (ii) противоречия в приоритетах; (iii) противоречия в профессиональном восприятии проблемы и в способах ее решения; (iṕ) угрозы профессиональной автономии органа и размывание границ ответственности и (ṕ) недостаточные знания органов друг о друге и о зонах ответственности. Приводится несколько процедур по преодалению этих сложностей, например, обеспечение гибкости и полной местной поддержки инициатив по профилактики преступлений, четкое определение ведущей роли каждого орагна, и привлечение профессиональных координатров для руководства программмой.

Оценка

Оценка программы является последним этапом профилактического процесса. По настоящее время этому аспекту не уделялось достаточно внимания в процессе профилактики преступности, и, по всей вероятности, этот элемент является наиболее трудноосуществимым с точки зрения достижения качественных результатов. Оценка чаще всего требует большого количества времени и средств, иногда процесс сопряжен с опасностью, но очено важно собрать данные о том, что и в каких обстоятельствах является эффективным. Оценка может быть разбита на две отдельные, но связанные друг с другом части - процесс и результат. Первое связано с наблюдением в ходе осуществления, второе - с определением степени влияния программы на уровень преступности и на другие факторы. Подробно описываются характер, сильные и слабые стороны наиболее последовательных научных методов оценки результатов - эксперементальный и квази-эксперементальный.

INTRODUCTION

Over the last two or three decades there has been an enormous increase in organised sets of activities which fall under the general heading of 'crime prevention' in Europe and North America. This has coincided with a substantial increase in crime in western societies during the same period and a number of attempts have been made to try to explain this increase. One explanation is that since the 1950s western societies have experienced significant social, cultural and economic changes, the most important of which are: the economic and social emancipation of an increasingly pluralist generation of young people; the erosion of formal socialising structures such as the family and the church; and the growth of consumerism along with heightened expectations of material well-being (Graham, 1993). These developments have led to marked changes in the 'routine activities' of everyday life which have created a proliferation of new and more suitable or attractive opportunities for crime, and a reduction in the number and capacity of capable guardians to protect these targets and exert a degree of informal social control (Cohen and Felson, 1979).

A second explanation, which is also based on an analysis of the changes which western societies have undergone in recent years, argues that late modern societies are characterised by 'localisation' (an unevenness in economic and social development leaving discrete locales with different market needs) and 'ontological insecurity' (fear generated by declining social structures and systems which provided security in the past) (Bottoms and Wiles, 1994). One result of these developments is a tendency in many urban areas for crime prevention to become localised and individualised within 'defended locales'. This has generated on the one hand 'pockets of security' which provide protection for those who have the power or resources to move to such areas, and on the other hand 'ghettoes of crime' in the non-protected areas of the city (Wiles, 1992). These trends have been exacerbated in some countries (most notably Britain and North America), where the role of the state has increasingly diminished and it has become accepted that neither the government nor the police can tackle crime alone. The phenomenon of localised and individualised crime prevention, which has become particularly marked in Britain and North America, has combined with a rapid expansion in the demand for private security, surveillance and patrolling services for the purposes of protection.

A third explanation is that during the 1970s and 1980s there was a rapid loss of faith in the ability of the criminal justice system to reduce crime or criminality. The findings of criminological research during this period were interpreted by some as showing that the criminal justice system was relatively ineffective in controlling the expansion of crime and the involvement of young people in criminal behaviour. It was believed that detection and conviction was largely ineffective in deterring the vast majority of offenders from committing further criminal acts (Steinmetz, 1982). The new era of police research conducted during the 1970s provided little evidence to show that the police were able to influence crime rates by changes in policing methods (Clarke and Hough, 1984). There was also little evidence to show that therapeutic and treatment regimes had any substantial effect in reducing re-offending among the bulk of people who attended them (Martinson, 1974). As a consequence of this loss of faith, it has been argued that governments and administrators began to look for alternative strategies outside of the criminal justice system to improve the efficacy of formal methods of control (Clarke, 1983).

These developments over the last thirty years provide the context within which countries have developed a wide range of policies and strategies for preventing and reducing crime. Such strategies vary in their extent and nature, often as a consequence of different perceptions of the crime problem and different explanations for the growth in crime. These different approaches are in turn reflected in different administrative and organisational arrangements for implementing crime prevention policies.

ORGANISATIONAL FRAMEWORKS FOR IMPLEMENTING CRIME PREVENTION

In some countries, such as Denmark, Sweden and the UK, specific policies for preventing crime have been an explicit part of criminal policy for at least two decades; in others, such as Germany, Austria and Switzerland, the concept of crime prevention as a separate and distinct aspect of criminal policy is still incipient. Most countries in Western Europe draw clear distinctions between crime prevention and the work of the criminal justice system, but in Eastern Europe the distinction is somewhat opaque. In, for example, Bulgaria, Hungary and the CIS, the courts take responsibility not only for adjudication, but also for identifying and resolving the underlying causes of specific offences. So, for example, where an offender is found guilty of theft from the workplace, the employer will be issued with a directive to prevent such thefts from recurring. Failure to comply can result in the employer being penalised. Thus the courts, rather than merely punishing offenders and relying on the principle of general deterrence to prevent others from committing similar offences, actively try to change the conditions and situations which generate criminal behaviour.

In Western Europe, some countries have adopted national strategies and have organised crime prevention through national crime prevention councils (e.g. France, Denmark, Sweden, Finland and Belgium). These tend to be fully or semi-independent bodies with membership being drawn from politicians, administrators, voluntary organisations, private industry, the police and the criminal justice system. In Denmark, for example, the National Crime Prevention Council, which was founded in 1971, comprises representatives from some 50 government and non-government organisations and is ultimately accountable to the Ministry of Justice. Other countries have organised crime prevention through inter-ministerial forums (e.g. England and Wales and the Netherlands) or individual ministries, usually of justice or the interior (e.g. Greece, Italy and Iceland). Inter-ministerial committees have the advantage of being able to coordinate the policies of other government departments with an interest in crime and criminality prevention (e.g. employment, housing, health, social services, education and transport) and monitor and assess the impact of their policies on crime. Others still have relied almost entirely on the role of the police and the independent activities of individuals and organisations (e.g. Germany, Austria, Switzerland and many of the Eastern European countries). Katona (1994) provides an overview of the administrative and organisational structure of crime prevention in 27 European countries. But one of the most elaborate frameworks has been set up in France, where a three-tier administrative structure has been set up at the national, regional and local levels.

The French structure is headed by a National Council for the Prevention of Crime, which consists of representatives from all relevant ministries and is accountable to the Minister of State for Cities. At the regional level, Departmental Councils for the Prevention of Crime, which are chaired by the chief administrator for the region, coordinate the implementation of national policies and at the local level Communal Councils for the Prevention of Crime are responsible for the practical implementation of crime prevention policies. The structure facilitates information exchange and the coordination of policy both horizontally - across local agencies and communities - and vertically - between local agencies and communities and central government (De Liege, 1988).

Communal Councils, which now exist in approximately four out of every five cities with more than 30,000 inhabitants (although some of these only exist on paper), are chaired by the local mayor (Graham, 1993). Members consist of elected officials, local administrators, members of the police and the judiciary and representatives of voluntary organisations, trade unions and the private sector. In large cities, Communal Councils are often created for each district and in more than 100 cities there are what are known as 'Missions Locales', which offer a wide range of services to young people at risk (see chapter 1). The Communal Councils organise local information campaigns which emphasise the common ownership of the crime problem and the importance of civic responsibility. Recently, Communal Councils have been encouraged to set up "observatoires", to provide information about crime and effective prevention programmes (Waller, 1991).

In addition to these national structures, there are pan-European organisations which promote the exchange of information on crime prevention policies and practices (e.g. the Council of Europe and the European Forum for Urban Safety) and recently an International Centre for the Prevention of Crime, which bridges the Atlantic divide, has been set up in Montreal, Canada. This Centre, which grew largely out of collaborative efforts between France and Canada, spans more than the interests of Europe and North America and includes as part of its remit the channelling of financial aid to cities in developing countries with an interest in preventing crime (Graham, 1993). This coincides with one of the principal aims of this book (and indeed the United Nations), namely to assist policy makers and practitioners in developing countries to select appropriate strategies and measures for preventing crime in their own cities.

DEFINING CRIME PREVENTION

There is as yet no universally accepted definition of crime prevention, or indeed any consensus on what crimes should be included in prevention programmes. Should white collar crimes such as company fraud, tax evasion and insider trading be included? Should traffic offences be included? Does crime prevention include the prevention of behaviours which cause a nuisance such as rowdyism among groups of youths, down-and-outs on the streets or even packs of dogs running wild on council estates? There are no agreed answers to these questions, but most existing experience in crime prevention, and most of the successes so far achieved, have been in relation to property offences, which in all countries form by far the majority of reported offences.

The situations in which offences such as theft, burglary and robbery are committed are similar from one country to the next, regardless of the stage of development or the cultural, legal or social system. However, attempts to prevent some of the more serious 'white collar' crimes are generally referred to specifically as 'fraud prevention' rather than under the general heading of 'crime prevention' and attempts to prevent some of the least serious crimes are generally referred to as 'problem solving' or 'disorder prevention'. Other crimes, such as environmental crime, traffic offences, sexual offences and offences against the state, are not commonly included in crime prevention initiatives and it was felt that drug and/or alcohol-related offending, which involve a different and more complex range of issues, could not be satisfactorily dealt with here. The first chapter however, which covers the prevention of criminality (the propensity of individuals to commit offences), has implications for the prevention of a broader range of deviant behaviour, including drug and alcohol related crime. Dryfoos (1990) shows clearly that the antecedents of a range of high-risk behaviours amongst adolescents (substance abuse, delinquency, adolescent pregnancy, school failure and drop out) overlap and that programmes to combat these high-risk behaviours have much in common. Thus the strategies and programmes in this book provide valuable insights into the prevention of mid-range 'street' crimes such as assaults, thefts, burglaries, robberies, auto-crime, criminal damage and arson, as well as other crimes commonly committed by young offenders.

Equally important is the requirement to define the parameters of prevention. Does prevention mean the elimination of crime? Clearly it cannot mean this in practice, even if this is considered an ideal goal to aim for. In one respect, it may be more appropriate to substitute the word 'control' for the word 'prevention. Thus crime prevention could be applied to attempts to 'control' or 'manage' the commission of crime and crime prevention could be considered as successful if offending rates decline or if the rate of increase in crime is less than it would have been without intervention.

There is also the problem of defining the broad area of activity covered by the concept of crime prevention. In practice, there are a number of current working definitions of crime prevention which cover different kinds of activity by different agencies. The broadest definition of crime prevention is one which encompasses any activity which reduces crime. Kaiser (1988), for example, defines crime prevention as including: '...all those measures which have the specific intention of minimising the breadth and severity of offending, whether via a reduction in opportunities to commit crime or by influencing potential offenders and the general public.' This definition might include the possible deterrent or preventive effects of imprisonment and other arms of the criminal justice system. It might also include other factors which contribute to crime rates but which are unrelated to the criminal justice system, such as improvements in the state of the economy. In this sense, crime prevention policy could even span economic policy. However, crime prevention is rarely, if ever, defined so broadly and it has been suggested that crime prevention, if only for pragmatic reasons, should be restricted to activities other than those undertaken by the criminal justice system (see, for example, van Dijk and Waard, 1991; Jeffery, 1977). In practice, it is difficult to exclude criminal justice agencies altogether, particularly the police, who clearly perceive the prevention of crime as one of their main functions.

Historically, crime prevention has developed in part as an antidote to the observed limitations of the criminal justice system to control crime. Furthermore, crime prevention is typically thought of as something which is 'pre-emptive' to the extent that it occurs before a crime has been committed. This definition could be challenged on the grounds that ultimately crime prevention strategies require the support or backup of the threat of sanctions offered by the criminal justice system. However, the literature on the deterrent, incapacitative, rehabilitative and treatment effects of the criminal justice system is so vast that it would be impossible to do justice to this wide range of material in a single volume. For largely practical purposes then, most western countries draw a clear line between the work of the criminal justice system and crime prevention, whilst acknowledging the importance of encouraging links between the two. This book follows this tradition, but includes the work of the police within its definition of crime prevention.

Tuck (1987), rather than attempting to reach an acceptable definition, suggests that crime prevention represents a way of thinking rather than any kind of definable action, and a shift away from traditional, formal methods of crime control and towards new, informal methods. This line of thinking has led, for the purposes of this book, to an approach which avoids pinning down crime prevention to a precise definition. Instead, the approach adopted here is to provide a logical and clearly understandable framework within which the activities generally referred to by policy makers and practitioners as constituting crime prevention can be classified.

CLASSIFYING CRIME PREVENTION

One of the earliest attempts to classify crime prevention activity was by Brantingham and Faust (1976). Their typology, based on a public health model of prevention, divides crime prevention activities into three groups: primary prevention, secondary prevention and tertiary prevention.

Primary crime prevention activity focuses on the physical and social environment and the factors which influence opportunities for crime such as environmental design, the natural level of security behaviour in the population, or levels of deprivation and poverty in residential areas. It is considered similar to primary prevention within the public health model which focuses on the disease creating conditions of the general environment, such as sewage treatment, mosquito extermination and small pox vaccinations. Primary prevention attempts to prevent the incidence of something by affecting the general environmental conditions which create it, rather than the individuals who might be affected by it.

Secondary crime prevention activity focuses on individuals, or groups of individuals, who are potentially at risk of becoming offenders. It aims to intervene in their lives in such a way that they never commit criminal violations. This might be done by supporting families at risk of breaking up, children at risk of educational failure or teenagers at risk of unemployment or homelessness. It is similar to secondary prevention within the public health model, which aims to intervene in relation to individuals or groups who have a high risk of developing a particular disease. This might involve chest X-rays in poor neighbourhoods, special diets for overweight executives and rubella vaccinations for prospective mothers.

Tertiary crime prevention activity focuses on individuals who have already committed offences and aims to intervene in their lives in a way which will stop them from committing further offences. This might be achieved through individual deterrence, rehabilitation, treatment or incapacitation. This is similar to tertiary prevention within the public health model which involves intervening in the lives of individuals who have already contracted the disease. This might involve surgery, therapy or rehabilitation.

However, this typology has been criticised on a number of grounds (see, for example, van Voorhis, 1986). While it usefully identifies the level of the action (i.e. at the level of the general environment, high risk groups, or actual offenders), it fails to take into account who does the action (e.g. police, community or potential victims) or the mechanisms by which the action is supposed to be effective (e.g. by increasing risk or reducing reward). There is also a problem of what to include in one category as opposed to another. In which category, for example, should the work of the police be placed? Some of the activities of the police could be considered as primary prevention (e.g. conducting security surveys and setting up neighbourhood watch schemes) whilst others could be construed as secondary prevention (e.g. running self-defence courses) or even tertiary prevention (victim support).

Most importantly the adoption of the public health model, which is grounded in the principles of pure science, implies that the causes of crime are as identifiable as the causes of disease. Social science is not an exact science. It deals largely with probabilities and correlates rather than certainties and causes. There are not only many competing theories about the causes of crime, but also inadequate or conflicting evidence as to the validity of these causes.

There have been several other attempts to classify crime prevention. Van Dijk and Waard (1991) have enhanced Brantingham and Faust's typology by adding an additional victim-oriented dimension whilst Ekblom (1994) has developed a 'mechanism-based' classification. The latter is based on the notion that crime can be prevented by manipulating the components of criminal events. He identifies three levels of activity: (i) the kinds of crime prevention method and the causal mechanisms it aims to influence, (ii) the target of the intervention in terms of whether it is the situation or the offender, and (iii) the types of crime which the strategy aims to prevent. Each of these main elements of the crime prevention process then become the subject of a separate system of classification, whose eventual aim is to systematically organise knowledge for practitioners and academics alike.

The most damaging criticism of many of the proposed systems for classifying crime prevention is that despite the fact that they are frequently cited in the academic literature, they are rarely used by practitioners (or even policy makers) as a working method for classifying crime prevention. Instead, policy makers and practitioners predominantly refer (albeit using slightly different terminology) to three main categories of crime prevention: criminality prevention (sometimes called 'social' or 'offender oriented' crime prevention), situational crime prevention and community crime prevention. These categories provide continuity with the classification system used in the first edition and are adopted in this book.

SCOPE OF THE BOOK

The main aim of this study is to review the design, use and effectiveness of the wide range of crime prevention strategies commonly adopted by countries in Europe and North America and, on the basis of this, to offer guidance to policy makers and practitioners, particularly in developing countries, on how to devise comprehensive strategies for preventing crime. Secondly it is also hoped that this book will be of use to academics and researchers involved in the study of crime and its prevention.

To assist in this, the findings of research and especially evaluative research, are drawn on extensively. Criminological research has made considerable advances during the latter half of this century and, in general terms, the factors which are strongly associated with either committing an offence or becoming an offender are, for most offences, quite firmly established. This has provided criminal policy makers with some scientific guidance for devising preventive measures. Many of the findings of research have also been tested in practice and evaluations of preventive initiatives have produced a much clearer picture of what works, under what conditions and why. Thus in describing various preventive approaches and measures, the book uses the findings of research and programme evaluations, including those which have been unsuccessful, to support and illustrate the value of such measures.

The book does not attempt to be prescriptive, but to document a wide range of programmes and their effectiveness as objectively as possible. The conditions relevant to understanding and preventing crime will tend to vary from country to country and different countries will place a higher or lower priority on preventing crime relative to other social problems. Implementing crime prevention measures can also be expensive and the costs of the programme need to be assessed alongside other factors in the decision making process. Caution should also be exercised in transferring programmes to other countries, particularly developing countries; the conditions between countries vary and not all initiatives, whether in part or as a whole, will be suitable in other environments.

In so far as crime in developing countries may be influenced by social and community disorganisation and economic disadvantage, the solutions may lie with efforts to ameliorate these conditions - i.e. with economic expansion, urban reconstruction and community rejuvenation. Some of the measures described in this book may be able to assist developing countries in combatting these conditions, but such processes are often highly complex and costly and results are only likely to be achieved in the long term. In the meantime, unacceptable crime and victimisation rates still characterise economically disadvantaged and socially disorganised communities. More immediate and pragmatic solutions which may alleviate crime rates in the short and medium term are also required. Here developments in Europe and North America in situational crime prevention may be of particular value. To the extent that different kinds of community require different solutions to their problems, developing countries may also be able to recognise features within these communities which are familiar to their own situation and adapt some of the community-based approaches to crime prevention described in this book to their own needs.

The following system of classifying crime prevention, which excludes the work of the criminal justice system but not the work of the police, has been adopted on the grounds that it is the most widely used, that it allows the inclusion of the greatest possible number of countries and the widest possible range of readership and ensures a degree of continuity with the classification system adopted in the first edition. The three chapters which cover crime prevention are: (1) criminality prevention, (2) situational prevention, and (3) community-crime prevention.

SOURCES OF INFORMATION

The information upon which the first edition of this book is based came from a range of different sources. A questionnaire was sent to experts in the field of criminal policy in every country in Europe and North America. The level of response to the questionnaire was high - thirty countries provided some form of response. However, the quality and depth of the responses was, by and large, disappointing. A few of the responses were followed up by visits, but it became clear that other sources of information would need to be tapped. The most fruitful source of information consisted of a thorough search of the literature, including on-line computer searches such as ICPIN (International Crime Prevention Information Network) and a two-week visit to the Max Planck Institute for International Criminal Law in Freiburg, Germany. Two conferences were organised at which experts from many UN member states made contributions on the structure and content of the report.

For the preparation of the first edition, a decision was taken to provide a document which contained the most innovative and advanced information on approaches and measures for preventing crime and this meant that it contained examples of programmes and initiatives from a relatively small and somewhat select group of countries - predominantly Canada, USA, Britain, France, Scandinavia and the Netherlands. This emphasis is also reflected in this second edition, which contains many new initiatives, particularly from Britain and the USA. The new material has been generated from literature searches and from short visits to France, the Netherlands and the USA.

THE STRUCTURE OF THE BOOK

The first chapter is concerned with criminality prevention (i.e. measures aimed at tackling the dispositions of individuals to offend). They may be targeted either at the general population or at specific groups or individuals at risk. The second chapter covers situational crime prevention and deals with strategies which aim to reduce opportunities for crime. The third chapter covers community crime prevention and is concerned with measures which aim to reduce crime at the level of whole communities. These may include strategies which aim to reduce criminality or to reduce opportunities for crime. The fourth chapter describes the process of preventing crime from the planning of initiatives through to their implementation and evaluation.

CHAPTER I. CRIMINALITY PREVENTION

I.I   INTRODUCTION

1.1.1   The reasons why people offend are complex and wide ranging. Tarling (1993) provides a useful recent summary of the factors associated with criminality, from early problem behaviour and family and school circumstances to the influence of peers and drug and alcohol abuse. Other more compre-hensive reviews, such as Rutter and Giller (1983), illustrate the whole range of influences on people's offending behaviour and in this chapter many of these influences are discussed in the context of preventive initiatives which their identification has led to. Two central constraints upon criminality are the amount and effectiveness of controls externally imposed upon, or internalised by individuals, which deter them from committing offences and the number of incentives to be law-abiding (i.e. the lack of opportunities for developing a personal stake in conforming to prevailing social norms). Both of these, along with the factors associated with offending identified by research on crime and criminality, are principal determinants of the dispositions of individuals towards offending.

1.1.2   The learning of norms and values and the provision of incentives to be law-abiding are generally transmitted through the major socio-economic structures and institutions of socialisation in society. Changes in the nature of these structures and institutions influence dispositions towards offending and ultimately crime rates. Criminality prevention therefore works by establishing how the nature of, and changes in, socio-economic structures and institutions of socialisation can promote dispositions towards offending and, where possible, altering them in such a way as to minimise or reduce such effects.

1.1.3   The negative impact of changes in the socio-economic structures and institutions of socialisation often falls disproportionately on specific sections within society, usually those least able to protect and insulate themselves from such changes - the young, the infirm, the immigrant, the poor, the unemployed, the homeless etc. Criminality prevention policies tend to focus on these groups, since they also tend to be the groups most at risk of offending, although strategies may also be targeted universally or on specific institutions or communities. But irrespective of targeting strategies, the prevention of criminality needs to feed into a wide range of social policies which have a bearing on crime.

1.1.4   It should be born in mind that social policy is and should be of value in its own right and should not be justified on the basis of its potential for preventing or reducing crime. Some may even question whether expending resources on, for example, supporting disadvantaged families, should be in any way dependent upon the prospect of future reductions in crime. Nevertheless, crime prevention through social policy is justifiable if the former is considered as just one of the possible outcomes of the policy.

1.1.5   In some areas, social policies may be considered important enough to warrant support despite a potentially criminogenic effect. Policies which, for example, withdraw financial benefits from certain sectors of society may result in the poorest resorting to some form of subsistence crime; the benefits in terms of financial savings may still be considered to outweigh the costs.

1.1.6   In other instances, however, governments may not be aware of the potential criminogenic effects of their policies. To minimise such effects, governments should be encouraged to monitor social trends and anticipate and assess the likely impact of new social policies on crime. Where social policies are enshrined in legislation, crime impact statements could be set alongside the financial and manpower implications of the new law. Social policies can also be scrutinised at the local level in terms of their potential impact on crime. Individual agencies can be asked to identify two or three policies which, over a period of time, are assessed and then revised to take account of any crimino-genic aspects and any potential for reducing criminality. The development of a system of crime impact statements should be seen, therefore, as a crime preventive policy in its own right.

1.1.7   Before discussing in more detail some of the measures which can be undertaken in the field of criminality prevention, it is important to point out how this approach differs from the other two approaches to crime prevention outlined in this report. The criminality prevention approach differs from situational and community-based crime prevention in at least three fundamental ways.

1.1.8   Firstly, criminality prevention inevitably focuses primarily on children and young people, since they are the principal targets of socialisation. Most adult offenders start committing offences as youngsters and so true prevention should start early to be of greatest benefit. This should not be limited to identifying young children at risk as early as possible in order to correct their behaviour before offending sets in. It should also focus on changing those organisational, institutional, structural and cultural arrangements in society which may adversely influence the socialisation of young people and increase their risk of becoming offenders later in life.

1.1.9   Secondly, different preventive approaches apply at different stages of social development. So, for example, family-based strategies will be very different for families with infants as opposed to teenagers and the kinds of preventive strategies which may be useful in primary schools may not be applicable in secondary schools. Similarly, employment and peer group based strategies will be more relevant to teenagers than to younger children, for whom the school and the family will constitute the most important areas of intervention. During the early years, when developmental changes are at their most rapid, parents need to be constantly up-dated through regular supplies of information, advice and support appropriate to each stage. Parents who know what to expect before each different stage are more likely to cope with the changes than those who are ill-prepared. This applies in particular to the teenage years, when a directory of relevant advice and support services tailored to different needs (single parents, step families, ethnic minority families) should be readily available.

1.1.10   Thirdly, criminality prevention cannot be so easily tested through project-based, short-term initiatives. It is a more long-term, programme-based approach and initiatives need to take root before they are likely to produce positive results. Criminality prevention is also very difficult to evaluate in terms of a direct impact upon area crime levels and most programmes only demonstrate success at the individual level. Since the relationships between offending and socio-economic structures and institutions of socialisation are highly complex, the effects of criminality prevention programmes may only be identifiable in terms of improvements in associated factors, such as aggressive behaviour, persistent truancy, educational performance and employment rates.

1.1.11   At least six areas of social policy are likely to contribute to the prevention of criminality - urban, health, family, education, youth and employment.

1.2   URBAN POLICY

1.2.1   Relevant areas of urban policy include slum clearance, housing management, homelessness, the design and provision of public facilities and shopping areas and the inter-relationships between the provision of housing and other services, especially transport and the location of employment. Policies on the design of the urban environment and housing management are covered in chapters 2 and 3 and youth homelessness is referred to in the section on family policy in this chapter. In general, however, the question of how urban (and rural) planning policies impact upon crime has still to be fully explored (but see Vahlenkamp, 1989) and while it is generally well known that large and overpopulated cities tend to suffer from higher crime rates than planned, low-density urban environments (see, for example, van Dijk et al., 1991), it is difficult to suggest practical policies which might relieve the effects of overcrowding in such cities.

1.2.2   Where possible, limiting the size and population density of urban communities through, for example, the use of 'green belts', should be encouraged, since research has shown that high concentrations of families with young children in residential blocks increases problems of supervision and informal social control (Foster and Hope, 1993). Thus policies which ensure a good mix of residents by age and family structure should be encouraged. Alternatively, improving the spatial organisation of existing urban populations in order to minimise segregation along class, race or other grounds may lead to reductions in criminality. In Chicago, for example, the Gautreaux project has attempted to increase the mobility of disadvantaged inner-city families by constructing policies and providing incentives for encouraging the integration of such families into suburban, non-disadvantaged neighbourhoods. According to the Eisenhower Foundation (1993), the Gautreaux project has been successful in improving the education, employment and economic circum-stances of such families, but no evidence is provided to support the implication that these gains have also resulted in reductions in crime and victimisation. But overall, there has been little exploration of the role of urban policy in reducing crime and criminality.

1.3   HEALTH POLICY

1.3.1   There is little evidence to suggest that those suffering from specific physical and mental disabilities are more predisposed to delinquency (Rutter and Giller, 1983). However, children with reading difficulties for example, may be at risk of school failure, which is a strong correlate of offending, so efforts to identify and remedy such difficulties may indirectly reduce the risk of subsequent delinquency. In so far as physical and mental disabilities may lead to a greater feeling of alienation and exclusion, community-based policies for ensuring the social integration of the physically and mentally disabled should be encouraged.

1.3.2   Similarly, the provision of comprehensive health care facilities may help to ease some of the burdens faced by multi-problem families and increase their ability to function more effectively. Policies at the national level to promote better health, nutrition and psychological well-being need therefore to be integrated and coordinated with health programmes targeted at those most in need at the local level. Barnum (1987) suggests that consistent and easy access to health services for children, particularly from lower socio-economic classes, is an important precursor of effective preventive care. Health service delivery, he suggests, could be enhanced by focusing on the varying health needs of children at different ages and delivering health services through schools, using outreach to involve families as and when necessary.

1.3.3   One of the most important aspects of health policy in relation to the prevention of criminality is policies concerned with drug and alcohol abuse. Dryfoos (1990) has assessed a wide range of substance abuse programmes in the USA and concludes that three types of interventions are most successful, although no single intervention or programme has been shown to reduce substance abuse in the long term. The three most effective approaches are school-based, social and life skills curricula using older children as role models, school-based individual counselling services and multicomponent, collaborative, community programmes. The prevention of substance abuse is a subject in its own right and cannot be comprehensively covered here, although in practice, many of the measures identified as successful in terms of preventing criminality referred to in this chapter will also influence propensities towards drug and alcohol abuse and related crime. (For a comprehensive overview of drug policies in relation to crime in Western Europe, see Albrecht and Kalmhout, 1990.) Another important aspect of health policy is that which is centrally concerned with improving the health and functioning of families rather than individuals.

1.4   FAMILY POLICY

1.4.1   The ability of families to function effectively is thought to be a crucial determinant in preventing delinquency. Research has shown that, along with good education and proper employment, stable and emotionally healthy families are powerful sources of effective socialisation and social integration (see, for example, Loeber and Dishion, 1983). The findings of longitudinal studies on child development have shown that early troublesome, dishonest and anti-social behaviour are important predictors of later offending and that the structure and functioning of families play a central role in determining the behaviour of children (West, 1982).

1.4.2   Whilst the nature of this notion of continuity between childhood troublesomeness and adult offending is still not clear - not all anti-social children become anti-social adults - an important way of preventing delinquency would nevertheless appear to be intervention within the family setting. It should, however, be stressed that there are limitations on the extent to which crime prevention policies based on supporting and working with families can be developed. Politicians and professionals are sometimes reluctant to interfere in what is a very personal and private area of life.

1.4.3   Those children who show signs of criminal behaviour at an early age are more likely to become serious, persistent offenders than those who begin offending in their mid-teens, who are more likely to grow out of crime (Patterson, 1994). Such children often come from families under severe stress characterised by multiple social and personal problems, discord and interpersonal conflict (Graham, 1988a; Rutter and Giller, 1983). In a meta-analysis of research carried out in America, Britain and Scandinavia (Loeber and Stouthamer-Loeber, 1986), four main clusters of family influences are identified as increasing the risk of offending:

- Neglect - where parents spend little time interacting with and supervising their children;

- Conflict - where parents exert inconsistent or inappropriate discipline and one party rejects the other;

- Deviant - where parents are themselves involved in offending and/or condone law-breaking;

- Disruption - where neglect and conflict arise from marital discord and the break up of the marriage, with the subsequent absence of one parent (usually the father).

1.4.4.   Of these four clusters of influence, neglect is the strongest and disruption the weakest. Where children experience a constellation of such adverse influences, the risk of becoming a recidivist offender responsible for a disproportionate amount of crime is at its greatest (Osborn and West, 1978). The key factor is the quality and consistency of relationships between children and their parents and, where two exist, between the parents themselves.

1.4.5   Family relationships can also be adversely affected by external influences. Multiply deprived, low-income families living in overcrowded and badly maintained housing in unstable communities are likely to experience much higher levels of stress, which in turn can adversely affect their capacity to bring up their children effectively. Lone parents are particularly vulnerable to such stresses and if they are also very young, socially isolated and dependent on welfare, the risk that their children will be socially maladjusted are greater still (Loury, 1987). However, separation or the fact of having only one parent need not necessarily predispose children to anti-social and delinquent behaviour. It is not the absence of a parent, but the quality and endurance of the child's relationship with the remaining parent which is important (Rutter et al. 1983).

1.4.6   A high risk background can be partly or wholly compensated by protective factors, which evolve at different stages of childhood development (Kolvin et al, 1990). For deprived boys in their first five years, an absence of over-crowding, small family size, effective mothering, good maternal health, good home care and employment of the breadwinner have been found to be important protective factors. For older boys, other protective factors become influential, such as good school performance, effective parental supervision, a good relationship outside the family and identification with positive peer-group activities. Thus different forms of intervention are likely to be more or less applicable at different stages of childhood development.

1.4.7   There are seven main forms of family intervention which can help to prevent crime: (i) preventing teenage pregnancy; (ii) the provision of pre and post natal services; (iii) providing education and guidance for parenthood; (iv) providing pre-school education for the children of disadvantaged parents; (v) providing support for families under economic and psychological stress; (vi) preserving families by avoiding the removal of a child into care and (vii) preventing youth homelessness. Most of the forms of family intervention discussed below do not explicitly aim to reduce criminality, but all of them target risk factors associated with criminality. The most successful interventions tend to be those which target more than one risk factor and are justified in terms of multiple outcomes.

(I)   PREVENTING TEENAGE PREGNANCY

1.4.7.1   Children born to teenage mothers are more likely than other children to experience poor health, low educational performance, cognitive and emotional difficulties and delinquency (Bright, 1992). Preventing school-age childbearing can be promoted through the widespread dissemination of information and advice on family planning, including confidential access to free contraception, and offering teenage mothers the necessary support and advice for enabling them to complete their schooling and avoid a second early pregnancy. There are, however, few programmes which have unequivocally demonstrated reductions in teenage pregnancies, at least in the USA (Dryfoos, 1990).

(II)   PRE AND POST NATAL PROVISION

1.4.7.2   Home visits from health workers during pregnancy and infancy whereby mothers receive advice on infant care and development have been shown to reduce criminogenic influences, such as child abuse and neglect during the early years, and the risk of later delinquency (Farrington, 1994). However in practice, it is very difficult to measure the effects of early interventions on later behaviour, particularly criminal behaviour. Despite the appearance of strong associations between early family variables and delinquency, there is a considerable body of evidence which suggests that the long-term, follow-up studies upon which these findings are largely based may be methodologically flawed (Rutter and Giller, 1983). Because of these difficulties, most early interventions focus on improving factors related to later delinquency, such as performance, behaviour and attendance at school, and behaviour in the home.

THE YALE CHILD STUDY CENTRE PROGRAMME, USA

The Children's House programme of the Yale Child Study Centre provides a wide range of services to small groups of low-income, urban families, including a high proportion of single parent families. Services are provided for two years from the birth of the first child and include paediatric care, visits by social workers to help mothers plan their budget, nutritional guidance, day care and assistance with links to other social services.

The programme was evaluated by matching 17 low-income families with control families selected on the basis of race, socio-economic status and the presence of a father in the home. The results showed that at age 13, members of the experimental groups performed and behaved better at school and were less likely to truant from school. Furthermore, mothers in the experimental groups reported fewer problems with the behaviour, discipline and supervision of their children than mothers in the control groups.

1.4.7.3 Given that school and family factors are potent predictors of delinquency, it would appear that the Yale programme reduced the risk of participants becoming involved in delinquency, although the number of participant families was too low for general conclusions to be drawn from it (Seitz et al., 1985). However, according to Zigler and Hall (1987), the money spent on services to each family has been more than matched by the money saved by schools in terms of poor performance and the provision of special remedial services. A similar programme, however, has demonstrated actual reductions in delinquency.

SYRACUSE FAMILY DEVELOPMENT PROGRAMME, USA

This programme provided pre- and post-natal advice and support to low income women through weekly home visits and free day care designed to develop cognitive and intellectual skills from 6 months to age 5. The programme was evaluated using a matched control group of children at age 3. Over 120 children were followed up to about the age of 15 and whereas 22 per cent of the control group had criminal records, only six per cent of the experimental group had been convicted of offences. Furthermore, the offences committed by those on the programme tended to be less serious than those committed by the control group and the girls in the programme attended more and performed better in school (Lally et al, 1988).

(III) PARENTAL GUIDANCE AND EDUCATION

1.4.7.4 The amelioration of children's troublesome and disruptive behaviour at an early age can also be fostered through effective supervision and discipline. Research suggests that parents should avoid erratic and inconsistent use of discipline, which prevents children from learning which forms of behaviour are acceptable to their parents (West, 1982). Parents need to be able to indicate clearly what constitutes acceptable and unacceptable behaviour and the allocation of resources for parent education and improving parenting skills can be of value in this respect.

1.4.7.5 Parenting courses can be useful for helping parents to recognise and respond more appropriately to family behaviours which may adversely affect children. They can be taught to respond more constructively, use discipline less harshly and more consistently and avoid situations which can precipitate discord. In practice, initial participation rates are often low and drop-out rates high, although both can be improved with financial incentives (i.e. larger family allowances).

1.4.7.6 Evaluations of some parent training programmes have shown limited success in reducing early disruptive and aggressive behaviour, such as the Oregon Social Learning Centre programme.

THE OREGON SOCIAL LEARNING CENTRE PROGRAMME, USA

One of the most meticulously evaluated parent training initiatives is the Oregon Social Learning programme, for parents of aggressive and delinquent children. Parents are trained to use positive, non-coercive methods of discipline, to deal consistently and decisively with anti-social behaviour, to negotiate acceptable standards of behaviour with their children rather than imposing such standards without consulting them, to develop problem-solving skills and improve communication and interaction within the family.

The Oregon programme resulted in reductions in aggressive behaviour by young children lasting up to one year and similar results have been recorded for stealing (Patterson et al. 1982), although again the effects were only short-lived. Unfortunately, a quarter of participating parents dropped out before completing the programme and a further quarter dropped out during the one year follow-up period. The short term improvements in the children's behaviour therefore have to be offset against the difficulties of maintaining parental motivation and the limited if not non-existent long term effects in terms of delinquency reduction.

1.4.7.7 The question as to whether reductions in aggressive behaviour during childhood also result in reductions in later delinquency is more difficult to establish. Certainly there is no evidence that training programmes for foster parents reduce the subsequent rates of the problem children in their care (Loeber, 1987). It is likely, however, that helping parents to listen to children, to monitor their whereabouts and behaviour and to exert consistent, non-violent discipline, will benefit family functioning. But the long term criminality prevention effects of parent training programmes for younger children with conduct disorders have yet to be firmly established.

1.4.7.8 Clinical interventions using parent training with the families of aggressive and behaviourally disturbed children tend to be intensive and expensive. It is not always easy to recruit and retain parents. Home visits combined with incentives and reminders can increase participation rates and by using experienced parents as volunteers, the take up of parent training and support services can be widened beyond those most in need. In the case of one such scheme in the UK (Gibbons and Thorpe, 1990), which uses volunteer parents to visit the homes of families with small children who are under stress, there is some evidence to suggest that such initiatives can prevent children being taken into care, which is known to increase the risk of later criminality (see below).

(IV)   PRE-SCHOOL EDUCATION

1.4.7.9 Pre-school programmes focus on improving the educational achievement, social competence and behaviour of young children from immigrant families, socially and economically disadvantaged families, or children with various difficulties. Most pre-school programmes do not explicitly set out to prevent later delinquency but are concerned with the more immediate objectives of improving the social competence and cognitive performance of participants. A well known exception to this is the Perry pre-school programme, which explicitly attempts to prevent later delinquency.

THE PERRY PRE-SCHOOL PROJECT, USA

The Perry pre-school project, which started in 1962, is the best known example of a pre-school project set up with the explicit objective of reducing the risk of delinquency. The project randomly allocated 123 black children from low socio-economic families to a pre-school child development programme and a control group (58 to the former, 65 to the latter) for a period of, in most cases, two years at the age of 3. Nearly half of the families were one-parent families and overall parents had low I.Q.'s, low levels of education, poor employment records and lived in over-crowded dwellings. The pre-school programme itself consisted of involving the children in the planning of classroom activities to promote their intellectual and social development. Teams of teachers were employed on very high pupil:teacher ratios for 2.5 hours per day for 30 weeks in each year. In addition, each mother and child received a home visit from a teacher once a week for approximately 1.5 hours.

Over a period of 16 years, information was collected for all children from the age of 3 to 11 and at the age of 15, 19 and 27. The information included data on, for example, school performance, attitudes, employment record and self- and police-reported delinquency.

THE PERRY PRE-SCHOOL PROJECT, USA
(continued)

The study, which was characterised by an unusually low attrition rate, found that those children who attended the pre-school programme performed better in school and adult education and were more likely to graduate and get employment. Teenage pregnancy rates were much lower - about half - and arrests rates were forty per cent lower than for children in the control groups at age 19. By age 27, about one in three of the control group had been arrested five or more times compared with about one in 14 of those who had attended the pre-school programme (Schweinhart and Weikart, 1993).

A cost-benefit analysis of the Perry pre-school project (Schweinhart, 1987) found that it costs in the region of $5,000 per child per year. A project run over one year will produce a sixfold return on the initial investment, whereas a two year project will be approximately half as profitable.

1.4.7.10 According to Schweinhart (1987) and the Canadian Council on Children and Youth (1989), the characteristics of effective pre-school programmes can be summarised as:

- Well qualified staff with special training in early childhood development, including an emphasis on the ability to change to meet the needs of children and their families as they become apparent;

- Child development-based curriculum, with clearly stated goals, which allows children to plan their own activities; goals should include the encouragement of independence, the development of self esteem and the teaching of problem-solving and task persistence skills;

- Careful support, management and evaluation of the curriculum;

- High teacher:pupil ratios (no more than 1:8), small classes (about 16 pupils) and preferably a two year minimum involvement for each child;

- Close collaboration of teachers with parents and the community, including close involvement at the programme design stage;

- Integration with other local resources and services, especially health, housing, education, social welfare and employment.

1.4.7.11 Although short-term effects are more likely than enduring effects, supplementing pre-school programmes with special socialisation and education programmes during the primary and secondary school years can help to enhance the possibility of attaining long term criminality prevention benefits. Also, one of the principal lessons gained from evaluations of early interventions of this kind is that a combination of family support and pre-school education is likely to be more effective than focusing on just the child or just the family (Yoshikawa, 1993).

1.4.7.12 According to the Canadian Council on Children and Youth (1989), a US Select Committee on Children, Youth and Families found that for every $1 invested in pre-school programmes, the return is $4.75 as a result of savings on special education, public assistance and crime. Given the relatively expensive initial financial outlay required for pre-school programmes, it would appear to be sensible to selectively target those most in need and most likely to benefit, such as those on child abuse registers.

(V)   FAMILY SUPPORT

1.4.7.13 There are certain developmental stages when families are naturally placed under greater strain (e.g. families with very young children or teenagers; families in the process of breaking up). Specific resources can be used to support families during such periods. Centres for providing counselling and advice for parents with teenagers and voluntary conciliation schemes for families in the process of breaking up are two examples. The former can help parents to understand and respond appropriately to the unique problems associated with adolescence, including how to help their offspring avoid negative peer group pressures. The latter can minimise the adverse effects of family break-up by helping all parties concerned to reach mutually acceptable agreements on access, custody and other complex family issues outside the sometimes damaging confines of divorce proceedings in court.

1.4.7.14 A range of family support systems can be developed to assist parents who have to deal with difficult behavioural problems, social isolation and family stress. Family support programmes, especially if they can provide links to other social services and informal neighbourhood resources, can improve school behaviour and performance, reduce child abuse and out-of-home placements to other forms of care, all of which are associated with an increased risk of offending (Graham and Utting, 1994; Bright, 1992). In addition to financial and material support, families can receive child care services, emergency day-care, health care, family planning advice, crisis intervention, counselling and temporary respite, especially for single parents. Open access family centres which provide creche facilities, playgroups, after school clubs and remedial services such as debt counselling and family therapy, may also bear on the prevention of criminality and more isolated families can be targeted through outreach workers, who can offer more informal advice on, for example, nutrition, parenting and home management skills. As yet, no family support programmes have demonstrated a direct impact on the future criminality of children.

(VI)   FAMILY PRESERVATION

1.4.7.15 The provision of child care by trained professionals can enable the identification of behavioural problems or child abuse at an early stage and provide an opportunity for offering informal child-rearing advice. Given the known links between childhood physical abuse and later offending (see Malinowsky-Rummell and Hanson, 1993), the prevention of child abuse can make a valuable contribution to the prevention of criminality. In extreme cases, child care workers may need to resort to care proceedings and a disproportionate number of serious offenders have spent at least part of their childhood in various forms of residential care (Walmsley et al, 1991). Good residential care can improve emotional stability and provide a stimulating educational environment, but all too often residential homes are unable to fully compensate for the emotional deprivation suffered by children who are separated from their families (Bullock et al, 1993). As a consequence, much existing childcare work is concerned with avoiding care proceedings where possible and family preservation services, which aim to avoid the removal of a child into care, may also reduce the risk of current or future offending.

TACOMA HOMEBUILDERS, USA

Tacoma Homebuilders uses professional social workers to provide intensive support and practical help to the families of children who are at imminent risk of being removed into care. Over a period of no more than six weeks, each social worker works with one or two families for up to 20 hours a week, calling on specialist services as required. At least 70 per cent of families have succeeded in staying intact for at least a year (Utting et al, 1993) and the cost savings are considerable. However, no evaluation data exists to determine whether the Tacoma programme has directly reduced offending.

1.4.7.16 In all cases where decisions are taken to remove children from their parents, those affected should have the right to be heard and to have their opinion taken seriously. Following this, efforts should be made to provide suitable alternatives, the most common of which is foster care. Unfortunately, the findings of research on the effectiveness of foster care are complex and equivocal. Whilst foster care for children in danger of physical abuse is, on balance, likely to be beneficial, foster care for children from families experiencing emotional difficulties may or may not be beneficial, depending upon a wide range of circumstances (Besharov, 1987). Moving children through a series of foster placements is, however, quite damaging and should be avoided. With respect to delinquency prevention, again the findings of research are equivocal (Hill, 1985).

(VII)   PREVENTING YOUTH HOMELESSNESS

1.4.7.17 Just as difficulties in the family can lead to a child being removed into care, so they can lead to teenagers leaving home prematurely. As a consequence, they may well become homeless and involved in crime, sometimes just to survive. Family and housing policies which minimise the risk and incidence of homelessness and policies which make provisions for those who become homeless are therefore important social crime prevention strategies.

1.4.7.18 Special youth centres with emergency shelter and access to longer term hostel accommodation as well as efforts to reunite runaways with their families and dissuade would-be runaways from leaving home, should form the main focus of a strategic response to runaways. Other services such as counselling, survival skills training and assistance with finding employment or alternative means of subsistence, should also be provided for runaways, preferably as part of a multi-agency response. In France, Foyers, which provide temporary shared accommodation for young homeless people without jobs, may offer a model for promoting self-sufficiency by providing a stepping stone towards independence. In England, the Crescent, a variation on the Foyer scheme, offers temporary accommodation and access to training, employment, educational opportunities and recreational activities to a similar client group. Young people aged 16 to 25 have to sign tenancy agreements and abide by "house rules", but as yet no information exists as to whether such schemes prevent or reduce criminality.

1.4.7.19 All too often runaways commit offences or come to the notice of the police in other ways and ultimately end up in court. The Prejop project represents an interesting attempt to divert runaways from court and care proceedings (see below). It is important that, taking into account the child's right to protection from abusive parents, reasons for leaving home must be carefully examined prior to any decision being taken on his/her possible return to the family home. Equally, if and when a runaway is picked up by the authorities, parents should have the right to be informed that their child is safe. Sensitive procedures for initiating and conducting parent/child reconciliation should be developed which ensure that neither parents nor runaways feel betrayed by those in authority.

THE PREJOP PROJECT, THE NETHERLANDS

Frequently, runaways and other young people at risk of offending are picked up by the police who, through no fault of their own, are limited in what they can do to help these youngsters. The Prejop project represents an attempt to overcome this difficulty by treating young offenders (other than recidivists) and children at risk of offending (especially runaways) as neglected and deprived and therefore in need of welfare assistance, rather than potential or actual offenders. The project consists of locating social workers in the immediate vicinity of local police stations so that they can provide immediate assistance in the form of crisis intervention. Internal case conferences are held every morning between the police and the social workers to establish appropriate referrals.

An evaluation of the project (see Graham, 1993) has shown that the scheme has improved parent/child and teacher/child relations in the short term, but has had no effects in terms of changing parental attitudes or improving levels of academic attainment.

THE PREJOP PROJECT, THE NETHERLANDS (continued)

However, comparing juvenile shoplifters who were referred to the project with a similar group not referred, it was found that the former were less likely to return to the notice of the police than the latter. Unfortunately this finding was not found for other offences, although shoplifting represented by far the largest offence category. It should also be mentioned that the samples were quite small - only about 7 per cent of all juvenile cases were referred over a period of ten months - and the follow-up period of six months was too short for the results to be conclusive.

1.4.7.20 The provision of accommodation and other services for runaways cannot make up for the loss of a stable family environment, but may go some way to compensate for such a loss. The extended family, which may consist of surrogate parents and use peer group pressure to exert discipline and control, can provide a sanctuary in which members can build new relationships, acquire a sense of self esteem and develop emotional and financial independence (see House of Umoja below). The essence of the extended family concept is to protect young people at risk by linking the stability of family life to the protective elements of education, training, employment and roots in the community, without the danger of institutionalisation or rejection by foster parents.

THE HOUSE OF UMOJA, USA

Set up in the late 1960s, the House of Umoja is a residential facility for young black offenders and high risk youth from the local community. The home, or 'sanctuary', is run on the principles of the extended family. The couple who run the home act as parents to all members, all of whom are perceived as 'brothers'. Each youth signs a contract which requires adherence to a strict sense of house rules, involves them in all aspects of the operation of the house (including chores) and ensures their participation in school. Members can receive individual counselling, advice on their educational needs, health check-ups, and assistance in securing employment or vocational training. But the main feature of Umoja is the way in which it fosters a sense of togetherness and mutual trust, both amongst members and between members and their house parents, within the context of the values inherent in African culture.

Members are expected to live independently after six months to one year of residence if family reunion is not a realisable goal. Ex-residents become 'old heads' who, together with current residents, use peer group pressure to help build self-respect, a sense of control and a willingness to channel personal resources into a future which revolves around education, employment and family. Youths are encouraged to set up various enterprises and Umoja has a removals company, a printing company, a restaurant, a security institute and a driving instruction enterprise. They provide some employment, but the majority seek jobs outside.

> ## THE HOUSE OF UMOJA, USA (continued)
>
> Success is measured in terms of the re-offending rates of adjudicated offenders who have lived in Umoja, which are very low, rather than rates of crime in the local community. But without control groups and reasonably large samples, it is difficult to assess the real value of this programme.

1.4.8   Family-based interventions can be offered universally, targeted on areas of high crime and social disadvantage or activated in response to referrals from official agencies such as social services. Universal services have the advantage of not stigmatising those who receive them as 'the families of potential criminals', but they need to be justified in terms of cost-effectiveness. One way to do this is to indicate the wide range of benefits in addition to criminality prevention of a particular programme, as many of the above examples illustrate. Targeting areas of high crime and social disadvantage reduces the costs inherent in universal provision whilst still avoiding the stigmatisation of individuals.

1.4.9   Research has found that young people who are poorly supervised by their parents are more at risk of committing offences than those who are more closely supervised (Wilson, H. 1980). Young males who spend considerable time with their peers and away from the supervision of their parents are particularly likely to offend (Riley and Shaw, 1985). Lone parents, particularly if they work full time, need special forms of support if they are to exercise the same degree of supervision over their children as two parent families. Parent watch initiatives (see chapter 2) can help to improve levels of supervision, particularly if they are well organised on a local community basis Supervision by other responsible adults can also help to reduce propensities to offend. Teachers and youth workers have an important contribution to make here, both of which are discussed in the next two sections.

1.5   EDUCATION POLICY

1.5.1   It is widely accepted that schools represent a powerful influence upon the young. Children spend a great deal of their formative years in various establishments designed specifically with their need for education and socialisation in mind. Schools therefore provide a promising focus of intervention and innovation and as institutions are more easily targeted than, for example, the family.

1.5.2   Schools offer opportunities for promoting social equality, cultural plurality and personal belonging, and help young people to acquire moral standards and social skills and a sense of responsibility as citizens. More specifically, they can provide pupils with information and guidance on the nature of delinquency and the importance of respect for the law, the implications of committing a crime, the workings of the criminal justice system and ways of preventing crime. Curriculum material for courses on the above is not difficult to find (see, for example, Graham, 1988b).

1.5.3   Overall, research does not provide conclusive evidence to support or refute the notion of a causal relationship between schools and delinquency. However, research does provide clear indications of how schools may inhibit or promote delinquency and hence how schools may be able to contribute to the prevention of crime. Through their capacity to motivate, to integrate and to offer pupils a sense of achievement regardless of ability, schools would appear to have a significant influence on whether or not pupils are drawn into the criminal justice system (Graham, 1992).

1.5.4   Pupils who fail or behave disruptively at school, or who persistently truant from school, are more likely to offend than those who do not. The causes of academic failure, disruptive behaviour and truancy are not entirely clear, but research suggests that schools themselves, whether primary or secondary, are largely responsible for these outcomes rather than the types of pupils who make up the school (Rutter et al. 1979; Mortimore et al, 1988). Therefore policies which influence the capacity of schools to minimise the occurrence of these three outcomes should form the central focus of school-based social crime prevention strategies.

1.5.5   There are many school-based initiatives which attempt to improve the academic performance or behaviour of individual pupils (see, for example, Hannon et al, 1991; Mortimore and Mortimore, 1984). The introduction of social learning and life skills courses into the school curriculum can increase the ability of pupils to anticipate and handle conflicts, including potentially criminal situations, and a number of initiatives have reported success in terms of enhanced academic performance and improvements in behaviour (see, for example, Kellam and Rebok, 1992; Reid, 1993). Successful programmes have also been introduced to reduce problems of absenteeism and declines in academic performance associated with the transition from primary to secondary school (see, for example, Felner and Adan in Pransky, 1991).

1.5.6   Children who learn to use aggression in social interactions are at risk of abusing the power it can confer on the user and in schools they may end up bullying other pupils. Research shows that bullying is strongly linked to later offending (Farrington, 1993), so efforts to reduce or prevent bullying in school will also contribute towards the prevention of criminality. An innovative scheme to use unemployed school leavers as mediators and supervisors in school has tried to reduce inter-pupil violence in schools in France.

THE SCHOOL SAFETY PROJECT, FRANCE

This project was set up to reduce bullying and violence in schools and increase road safety on the way to and from school. Unemployed youngsters without qualifications and with a somewhat jaundiced view of teachers and schooling are employed as mediators/supervisors. Recruits are given an eight day training programme on issues concerning children and adolescence, including drug taking, deviant behaviour and road safety. Recruits are contracted to schools for six month periods, during which they receive on-the-job training. Their work varies from helping teachers with their supervisory tasks during lunch breaks and after school, to mediating between pupils involved in fighting or bullying. Schools which have employed recruits have reported marked reductions in violence and improvements in teacher/pupil relations (King, 1988), although the evidence in support of these findings falls short of scientifically rigorous standards.

1.5.7   The most effective approach to reducing or preventing bullying is the so called "whole school" approach developed in Norway. The main components of this approach comprise raising awareness about the problem of bullying amongst teachers, parents and pupils, involving them in the formulation of anti-bullying policies and ensuring the school creates a climate in which incidents of bullying are readily reported and takes full responsibility for prioritising and implementing anti-bullying strategies.

ANTI-BULLYING INITIATIVE, NORWAY

Following the introduction of a national campaign to reduce bullying in schools in Norway, in which schools and families were given information and advice on how to reduce/prevent bullying, an evaluation of the effects of this programme was conducted, using a quasi-experimental design, in 42 schools in the town of Bergen. The programme had four main goals: to increase awareness of the problem of bullying, achieve active involvement on the part of teachers and parents, develop clear rules against bullying behaviour and provide support and protection for victims. A series of measures were introduced at the school, class and individual level, such as devising specific rules about bullying, inserting discussions on bullying into the curriculum, encouraging victims to report incidents of bullying and introducing better systems of playground and after school supervision.

In addition to its effects on bullying, the evaluation also measured its effects in terms of reductions in crime (vandalism, theft, burglary and fraud) and anti-social behaviour in school. The findings are encouraging, with marked reductions in the levels of bullying and victimisation both in and to a lesser extent outside school, as well as reductions in crime and anti-social behaviour, in both the short term (after eight months) and the longer term (after 20 months). These findings were also found to be due to the programme itself and no evidence of displacement was identified (Olweus, 1991).

1.5.8   Interventions which target high risk individuals on the basis of behavioural, cognitive or educational deficits rarely produce *enduring* effects, whether individual- or classroom-based (Kazdin, 1993). Programmes which focus on the social interactional context within which a child behaves tend to be more effective, but such interventions rarely have an impact beyond the arena in which they are implemented and have not been found to reduce or prevent delinquency. As with anti-bullying initiatives, the most promising approach to criminality prevention in schools is also the 'whole school' approach, which focuses on changing the organisation and 'ethos' (the history, values, attitudes and practices which in combination, give it a unique atmosphere or climate) of schools. According to the US Office of Juvenile Justice and Delinquency Prevention's comprehensive review of the effectiveness of a wide range of delinquency prevention programmes, school-based programmes which focus on selective organisational change were not only considered the most promising, but offered broad and lasting benefits at a moderate, non-recurring cost (Office of Juvenile Justice and Delinquency Prevention, 1981).

1.5.9   Social interaction within the school, the school's values and its organi-sational structure represent the focus of such change strategies. A number of features of schooling have been identified by research as important constituents of effective schools. In essence, it is what is taught, how it is taught, how pupils and teachers relate to one another and how pupils are rewarded and disciplined, which determines whether a school is effective or not.

(i)   What is taught

The relevance of, the degree of academic content in, and the demands made on pupils by the school's curriculum all affect pupil motivation. The curriculum should be balanced in terms of academic and practical content so that it reflects the needs and abilities of the pupils. Low ability pupils should receive opportunities for developing their social skills, acquiring work experience and involvement in local community activities. The curriculum should be wide-ranging, flexible and, above all, stimulating.

(ii)   How it is taught

Teachers should be well prepared for lessons, select their material in accordance with the cultural and academic diversity of their pupils and   develop effective instructional and class management skills.

(iii)   Teacher/pupil relations

As well as building up mutual trust and respect, teachers need to learn   how to correctly handle conflicts, both between pupils and between pupils and themselves. They should learn how to avoid confrontations, how to foster initiative and imagination and has to allow for the developing adult status of older pupils.

(iv)   Rewarding and disciplining pupils

Just as bad behaviour needs to be punished, so good behaviour needs to be rewarded. But it is not so much what rewards and sanctions are used (although corporal punishment is generally considered to be ineffective if not counter-productive), but the overall style of rule enforcement. Rules need to be clear, predictable and immediately and consistently enforced, but within an overall context of tolerance. The process of disciplining pupils should not become the separate responsibility of specific teachers or the head teacher, but should be the responsibility of all teachers.

1.5.10   Effective schools are those with high levels of commitment and pupil participation, where all pupils succeed in some way or another, where teachers and pupils like and trust one another, where rules are clear and consistently and fairly enforced and where schools accept full responsibility for looking after as well as teaching their pupils. Schools which successfully motivate, integrate and reward their pupils, irrespective of social class, ethnic origin or academic ability, are likely to contribute the most to preventing crime.

1.5.11   Schools which are likely to have high rates of delinquency among pupils are those which, inadvertently or otherwise, segregate pupils according to academic ability, concentrate on academic success at the expense of practical and social skills, categorise pupils as deviants, inadequates and failures and refer responsibility for the behaviour and welfare of their pupils to outside agencies and institutions. Schools which permanently exclude their most difficult pupils or ignore those who persistently fail to attend school, may themselves be contributing to the promotion of delinquency.

1.5.12   A range of additional measures can assist schools in their responsibility for fully integrating those most at risk of offending - the persistent truants, the failures, the most troublesome. Schools should be informed of known truants and special re-integration programmes should be devised to coax school refusers back into school. Locally-based teams of peripatetic teachers skilled in work with difficult children should be made available to schools to help them resolve problems of disruptive behaviour within the school or the classroom at the earliest possible stage. It is important that, as far as possible, disruptive behaviour is tackled without scapegoating the child and within the context in which it arises. In some cases, schools may need to review their own organisation and 'ethos' with a view to changing internal conditions which give rise to truancy and disruptive behaviour.

1.5.13   As part of a major initiative to combat delinquency, the US Office of Juvenile Justice and Delinquency Prevention funded seventeen diverse, school-based programmes under their Alternative Education Initiative. This initiative sought to reduce delinquency by, amongst other strategies, strengthening pupil commitment, increasing active participation in school activities, offering pupils a greater stake in their school, ensuring all pupils experience success at school and encouraging attachment to conforming members of the school community. The PATHE project (Positive Action Through Holistic Education), constituted one of these projects.

THE PATHE PROJECT, USA

The PATHE project combined planned institutional change with individually-based initiatives to increase educational attainment and reduce delinquent behaviour. It sought to reduce delinquency and school disorder by changing the school climate with a view to decreasing academic failure experiences, increasing social bonding and improving pupils' self concepts. These objectives were to be achieved by encouraging mutual respect and co-operation and a sense of belonging amongst all school members; improving communication and encouraging a high degree of pupil and staff participation in the planning and implementation of change; providing clear, fair and consistently enforced rules and improving teachers' class management skills.

THE PATHE PROJECT, USA (continued)

The programme had five major components:

- The setting up of teams of pupils, teachers, parents, school administrators and representatives from community organisations to review, revise and implement changes in the curriculum and disciplinary matters.

- The introduction of academic innovations to improve attitudes to testing and study skills, including team learning, which enhances self concept and school attachment.

- The introduction of measures to improve the school climate, such as running a School Pride Campaign and providing pupils with a forum to discuss issues of concern.

- As children enter adolescence, parents need to recognise and acknowledge their emerging adult status and in doing so adopt a more conciliatory approach to the negotiation of rules and expectations, particularly with respect to the setting of boundaries to their newly emerging personal freedom. Making improvements to the transition from school to career and post-secondary education, including training in skills for finding and keeping jobs.

- Providing special academic and counselling services to pupils with academic/behavioural problems.

The programme was conducted in eight, predominantly black, inner city schools, two of which acted as controls. With pre- and post-reorganisation tests, each school also acted as its own control. The fifth component was evaluated by true experiment (i.e. identified pupils were allocated on a random basis to treatment and control groups). Data on a wide range of indicators, including delinquency and school behaviour, were collected from official records and self-report surveys.

The results show that the institutional change elements of the project had a small but measurable effect on delinquency and school behaviour. Similar improvements were not recorded for academic performance, attendance and self-concept. However there were improvements in attachment to school, staff morale, school safety and rule enforcement. In contrast, the individual measures had no effect on delinquency, attachment to school or pupil self-concepts, but did produce small improvements in attendance and academic performance. Unfortunately, information was only collected *during the course of the project,* so no information is available on whether the identified improvements continued *beyond* the project's duration (for a detailed account of this and other projects funded under the Alternative Education Initiative, see Gottfredson and Gottfredson, 1986).

1.5.14   The structures and processes which characterise large organisations are inherently complex. The difficulties involved in setting up and implementing organisational changes in schools are thus numerous and considerable. Factors which facilitate change will include:

- the attitudes, especially the willingness to change, of school heads and senior staff;

- the policies of public education authorities;

- the capacity of teachers to work together as a team;

- direct involvement of staff, pupils and parents;

- the achievement of the correct balance between stability and change;

- setting and maintaining realistic expectations.

1.5.15   Changing schools to prevent crime cannot be justified on the grounds of delinquency prevention alone, but must be part of an initiative to improve the school in all respects. Sometimes school priorities for improvement may even conflict with the objective of preventing crime. Such questions of priority and competing interests can only be resolved within the broader domain of public and political discourses on precisely what is expected of schools.

1.5.16   One of the principal findings to emerge from research and evaluation in the field of child development is that the prevention of adverse outcomes, be they substance abuse, teenage pregnancy or criminality, requires a continuum of intervention throughout childhood, incorporating work with both families and schools. Given that parental attitudes to education in general and their children's school in particular are important determinants of academic achievement and rates of absenteeism (Utting et al, 1993; MVA Consultancy, 1991), close links between families and schools need to be sustained and strategies for encouraging parents and teachers to support one another should be developed. In Sweden, home:school partnerships promote parental involvement in schools by encouraging parents to participate directly in classroom activities. In England and Wales, home:school agreements are used for setting the boundaries of acceptable behaviour and preventing incidents of unacceptable behaviour. In the USA, a number of initiatives for promoting home:school partnerships have been developed.

LIFT, USA

The LIFT (Linking Interests of Families and Teachers) programme was set up in Oregon to prevent conduct disorders. The main strategy consists of encouraging pro-social and discouraging anti-social behaviour at home and at school through parent training, social skills class for children, measures to improve behaviour and supervision in the playground and the use of a school-to-home telephone line on which teachers and parents can leave and receive messages. Initial findings suggest that LIFT has reduced aggressive and anti-social behaviour in the short term (Reid et al, 1994).

1.5.17   Partnerships between parents and teachers which integrate parents into the life of the school and offer both parents and teachers an opportunity to construct a joint approach to socialising the children in their care could produce a greater impact on criminality prevention than targeting families and schools in isolation (Graham and Utting, 1994). Delinquent peer groups develop in local communities and/or in local schools and together parents and teachers are likely to be able to exercise more effective control and supervision of groups of young people than apart. Families and schools are part of communities and any criminality prevention strategy which focuses on these two institutions of socialisation should also be part of a wider, multi-agency approach which draws on and incorporates the resources of the local community. This is taken up further in chapter 3.

1.6   YOUTH POLICY

1.6.1   Whilst the family and the school are undoubtedly the most important influences on a young person's likelihood of offending, there are limits to the extent to which parents and teachers can exercise effective supervision over children's lives. Riley and Shaw (1985) found that offending is associated with the amount of spare time boys spend away from home with their friends. This suggests that supervision in such circumstances by responsible adults (other than parents), might be able to make a valuable contribution to the prevention of male juvenile offending. Outside schools, youth workers represent the most likely source of additional supervision, particularly in public places.

1.6.2   The main objective of youth work is to secure the personal development of the individual through social education, a crucial component of which is to encourage young people to take responsibility for their own lives. Young people should therefore be offered as much scope as possible to participate in and take responsibility for the activities they engage in. Whilst it can be difficult to maintain a balance between exercising a degree of restraint and allowing young people to manage their own affairs in their own way, it is important that they learn to take responsibility for their own actions, including those which amount to breaking the law.

1.6.3   There has been little systematic research on the potential influence of youth work in general on crime, whether in terms of overall levels of provision or specific interventions. Little is known about which kinds of provision are most likely to attract or repel those young people most at risk of offending and there is no evidence that providing youth clubs on housing estates reduces crime or criminality (Baldwin and Bottoms, 1976; Graham and Smith, 1993). Similarly, there has been little research on the preventive effects of other forms of youth work, such as information, counselling and advice centres, drop-in centres, skills centres and detached and outreach work (but see below). However, with the greater exposure of young people to periods of under/unemployment during the transition to adulthood, the provision of cultural and leisure activities has become increasingly important. With limited opportunities for making decisions and taking responsibility in the world of work, young people need to be offered alternative ways of acquiring independence and maturity. Equally, if there are not adequately developed, directed and supervised play facilities, play may become distorted into vandalism, shoplifting and other forms of juvenile crime.

1.6.4   The importance of providing diverse and imaginative forms of leisure and cultural activity in a world which increasingly values and encourages passive consumption and creates for many young people unattainable expectations, should therefore not be underestimated. Young people need to feel they are useful, appreciated and of value. Special projects initiated and managed by young people themselves can help them gain a sense of self-esteem and independence. Activities such as sport, music, theatre, dance and literature, can all help young people to gain insights into themselves, their worth and their ability to relate to others. Such activities can also help to counter ethnic and racial ignorance and prejudice and to integrate young people into the wider community. In France, a scheme for providing a wide range of activities for young people during the summer holidays was introduced as part of wider programme concerned with preventing crime and integrating marginalised young people.

THE ETE-JEUNES PROGRAMME, FRANCE

Centred on the long summer holidays during which levels of formal supervision are at their lowest, this programme encompasses a wide range of activities for young people. The central principle which guides the ete-jeunes programme is that the activities, which range from sporting and outward bound activities to discos and open-air film shows, is that the activities should, as far as possible, represent the interests and wishes of the young people themselves rather than being imposed upon them. Special summer activities passports can be purchased for a nominal fee by those under 25 years of age to cover all the activities on offer. The use of passports enables programme organisers to monitor levels of participation and pinpoint areas where ete-jeunes has failed to penetrate. 'Animateurs' have been employed to stimulate and direct participation in some of the activities, such as camping holidays, and to integrate young offenders under supervision orders with other participants.

A central thrust of the ete-jeunes programme is to integrate marginalised and ethnic minority groups into 'main-stream' social and sporting activities. The aim is to penetrate and target immigrant populations without threatening or undermining their cultural and religious identity. This has been assisted through the recruitment and incorporation of local ethnic minority gang leaders as animateurs and youth workers. Unfortunately, there is no information on the extent to which the ete-jeunes activities are successful in targeting marginalised and disadvantaged young people.

Compared with previous years, levels of reported crime fell over the summer months in those cities in which ete-jeunes activities were originally introduced. However, it is not known whether this is directly attributable to the activities or other factors. In many cases the activities are more concerned with improving social and racial integration and building self-confidence and a positive self-image rather than crime prevention. Indeed more recently, there have been suggestions that most programmes no longer contain activities explicitly aimed at preventing crime (Dubouchet, 1992).

1.6.5   According to Krikorian (1986), one of the strands of thinking behind this approach to assimilating marginalised groups of immigrants and young people is that both experience transitional problems of adaptation, albeit for different reasons. Immigrants (or migrants for that matter), have to adapt to strange cultural conditions and sometimes hostile social attitudes. Marginalised youth (or in some cases those who are not marginalised), have to adapt to the demanding expectations of adulthood, often without the necessary skills or resources for doing so. Both groups must find ways of successfully bridging a stage of transition not of their own making. The most difficult problem associated with integrating marginalised people is therefore firstly to reach them, secondly to build up a trusting relationship with them and thirdly to then do something about meeting their needs and resolving their problems - to help them cross the bridges they are confronted with. Failure to do so may result in some turning to crime as an alternative solution.

1.6.6   Despite the common belief that diverting youthful energy into creative, constructive and legitimate activities reduces boredom and a tendency to engage in illegal or criminal activities, there is little empirical evidence in support of this belief. What evidence there is suggests that the impact, if any, is likely to be no more than quite minimal (Graham and Smith, 1993). The integration of marginalised young people into the community is unlikely to be successful without attempts to influence their economic, social and material circumstances. Efforts to provide imaginative and constructive leisure activities therefore need to be supplemented with efforts to provide the means of securing emotional and financial independence. In the Netherlands, a national network of youth centres provides services for young people who are experiencing difficulties in acquiring the means for achieving such independence.

SOSJALE JOENITS, THE NETHERLANDS

In the Netherlands, some 60 youth advisory centres (Sosjale Joenits) exist throughout the country. They offer advice and support to young people between 11 and 25 (most are between 16 and 20) on matters relating to housing, employment, education, training, social security and drugs and alcohol problems. They adopt a child-centred approach, work closely with the police and target their resources in particular on runaways, the unemployed, the homeless and other young people at risk. They are concerned with helping young people to help themselves so that, for example, runaways who come to the centres for accommodation are required to participate in a survival skills training course before they are accepted in hostels. The emphasis is on teaching young people how to make decisions for themselves and live with the consequences, how to gain self-confidence and self-esteem, and how they are worthy in spite of their limitations and the difficulties they may face. As in France, the Dutch youth centres adopt the approach of trying to integrate young people into a society or community from which they feel estranged or rejected (Junger-Tas, 1988). No data exists, however, on their capacity to prevent crime and criminality.

1.6.7   The provision of youth centres may not be sufficient to reach and build up relationships with the most alienated young people and those most at risk of offending. Outreach or detached work can be very successful in terms of contacting and developing relationships with the most marginalised young people. Since research has shown that detached youth work can improve levels of social adjustment, it may have an important indirect influence on the propensities of some young people to offend. A review of early juvenile delinquency prevention experiments by the U.S. Department of Justice reported only one effective project out of the ten considered. This was the Wincroft detached youth work project, which ran during the mid-1960s and today still represents one of the few relatively successful examples of youth work oriented delinquency prevention initiatives.

THE WINCROFT PROJECT, ENGLAND

The Wincroft project consisted of detached/street workers whose main function was to contact and develop relationships with young offenders living in a working class, high crime neighbourhood. The project was evaluated in terms of the social adjustment and delinquent activities of the young people it reached. A target group of 54 boys with an average age of 15 was compared with a control group of 74 boys over the project period of 31 months. A follow-up study twelve months later offered an indication of whether any benefits the project may have had were sustained after it had ceased. The results are quite encouraging.

Comparisons between the target and control groups showed statistically significant differences between the two groups. The target group fared better than the control group in terms of the number of court appearances, convictions and self-reported offences committed during the period of the project. From an examination of police records one year after the project had ceased, the target group still had less contact with the criminal justice system than the control group and were still committing fewer offences. However, they were committing more offences than before and the offences they committed tended to be of a more serious nature. This suggests that the project acted as a holding operation for some, but with behaviour tending to deteriorate after the project had ceased.

The evaluators found that the benefits of the project were greatest for the least disturbed boys. This might be taken to suggest that such initiatives should be targeted at those at risk of offending rather than convicted delinquents. This inference should, however, be treated with caution, since the Wincroft Project was only targeted at convicted offenders (Smith et al 1972). (A similar study by O'Donnell et al.(1979), which included target and control groups of non delinquents as well as delinquents, found that whilst the delinquents benefitted more than the delinquent control group, the non delinquents did not. Indeed the non delinquent target group fared worse than the non delinquent control group.)

1.6.8   Sometimes young people's leisure facilities are the streets and shopping centres of towns and cities. With nothing to do and nowhere to go, they often end up attracted by the bright lights, the lavish displays of consumer goods or just the prospect of shelter from the cold. In some shopping areas, this can lead to the potential for continuing, low-level friction between the young people hanging around and those using the shopping centre for more legitimate purposes, including shopkeepers and security guards. Here too detached youth workers can prove useful in preventing crime. A more recent detached youth work project, which is more focused than the Wincroft project, targets young people who hang around shopping centres.

THE ROTTERDAM SHOPPING CENTRE PROJECT, THE NETHERLANDS

A study of crime in two shopping centres in Rotterdam showed that half of all crime reported to or registered by the police were committed on members of the public (Colder, 1987). The most common offences were street robbery, pickpocketing, theft from cars and of bicycles. The usual response to shopping centre crime is to use police patrols, security guards, store detectives and various forms of technical surveillance. But this project departed from this approach by attempting to integrate potential offenders rather than protect goods and property.

A crime prevention commission, with representatives from the municipality, the police, the public prosecution office, a youth organisation and a shopkeepers association, appointed a detached street worker to set up and co-ordinate the project. The police issued a special circular, which set out the rules of behaviour governing conduct within the confines of the shopping centre. These rules were circulated to all secondary schools in the vicinity and the police held discussions during which the rules, and the consequences of breaking them, were explained.

The aim of the project was to promote harmony between shopkeepers, young people who hang around the shopping centre and the shoppers themselves. Rather than excluding young people from the shopping centre or moving them on, specific places were provided where young people could freely congregate. Funds were provided for organising sports and leisure activities, particularly during week-ends and the holiday periods, and the detached worker successfully negotiated employment in the shopping centre for a few young people. According to Junger-Tas (1988), damage from vandalism and losses from shoplifting both declined following the introduction of the project, but it is not known if these effects were sustained in the long term.

1.6.9   Older teenagers commonly use a variety of entertainment outlets during the evenings, often in the centre of cities, to meet and drink with their friends, to seek excitement and to make contact with members of the opposite sex. Problems associated with noise, alcohol and drug consumption and disorderly behaviour are not uncommon. Hope (1985), in a policy analysis of drinking and disorder in city centres, lists a number of situational and managerial measures which can be taken to reduce city centre disorder (see chapter 2) and points to the importance of involving a wide range of interested parties and co-ordinating their knowledge and expertise. In France, the European Forum for Urban Safety, which organises exchange programmes for European cities, has set up a project to deal with some of the problems associated with city centre night life.

1.6.10   By identifying and working with natural peer groups at risk of offending and keeping in close touch with local schools, parents and a range of community and other agencies, including the police and representatives of the judiciary, youth workers and youth organisations can play a more central role in the integration of young people into the community. Increasingly work with young people is located within a locally based, multi-agency network, which provides access to a range of resources which can alter the socio-economic conditions affecting their lives and their dispositions to offending. In Denmark, the National Crime Prevention Council has set up a number of standing committees for preventing crime in most local municipalities. One such committee, the SSP committee, has the task of preventing crime by young people.

DECIBEL, FRANCE

Delegations from eight European and North African countries, consisting of politicians with an interest in young people's affairs, disk jockeys, education-alists, youth workers and representatives of the music business, were brought together by the European Forum to develop preventive measures associated with the use of night time entertainment by young people. The first stage - a three-day meeting - was used to discuss the nature and scale of the problems associated with night life, such as excess noise, traffic accidents, excessive alcohol consumption, drug abuse and disorderly behaviour, and to exchange ideas on preventive measures. A number of ideas were canvassed, including:

- providing music writing and choreography laboratories for young people;

- reducing alcohol-related crime by providing transport and emergency overnight accommodation for excessive consumers of alcohol, banning the sale of alcohol one hour prior to closing time in bars and discotheques, putting on alcohol-free events and administering anonymous alcohol tests at the exits of entertainment establishments;

- ensuring low level police presence and encouraging entertainment establishments to employ and train their own professional security personnel;

- soundproofing discotheques or locating them away from residential neighbourhoods;

- setting up local commissions comprising partners involved in the entertainment world to co-ordinate preventive measures.

DECIBEL, FRANCE (continued)

Although it is not yet known how well Decibel will perform, it is an imaginative example of how international collaboration can be used to generate preventive programmes.

1.6.11   Detached or street workers, or their equivalent, are often best placed to discover the precise needs of young people without compromising the principles of trust and confidence. They are able to contact groups of young people where they naturally congregate and develop trusting relationships before encouraging them to take part in small group work or specific activities. They are often in a position to know better than any other agencies what the precise needs are of the young people with whom they are in touch and are therefore well placed for mediating between them and the network of local services. To assist in this process, small local surveys can be carried out on the local social and economic situation of young people prior to devising an overall strategic response to their needs and problems. This approach has been admirably attempted in the city of Wolverhampton in England.

THE SSP COMMITTEE, DENMARK

Headed by four local Department chiefs - Police, Education, Social Services and Cultural Affairs - the SSP committee has responsibility for identifying local needs, devising strategies of prevention, targeting resources and co-ordinating the implementation of activities. Other committee members include representatives of sporting facilities, youth clubs and tenants' associations. The main focus of the committee's work is on creating a support network of parents, teachers, youth and community workers, social workers and police officers for young people 'at risk'.

The SSP committee sets up project groups to deal with specific community problems. In the city of Aarhus, for example, criminal behaviour by a group of young adults was causing considerable concern in one area of the city. Levels of fear were high, younger children were beginning to emulate their older peers and both crime and levels of fear were spiralling. The SSP committee made contact with the older group first, giving them the opportunity to set up their own youth club. Through this, they began to feel less isolated from the community, started behaving differently and as a consequence the younger children began to emulate more constructive role models. An inter-agency initiative was established to focus on the more important needs and problems of this group and gradually the conditions were created in which the conflicts facing these young adults could be confronted and resolved (Jensen, 1988).

There are no data available as to how successful this initiative is, or indeed SSP committees as a whole are in dealing with crime and fear of crime. Evaluation has rather tended to focus on the overall implementation process, which has experienced a range of difficulties. In Aarhus, initial mutual distrust between agencies - the police, the education authority and the social services - severely restricted their capacity to co-operate with one another and create a joint strategy. Expectations of one another were often unrealistic, agency representatives tended to work on the basis of very different principles and objectives and a general lack of consensus severely hampered the development of early initiatives.

THE SSP COMMITTEE, DENMARK (continued)

To resolve some of these difficulties, a series of seminars were held and a steering committee was set up to identify mutual problems, monitor and evaluate programmes of action and generally act as a resource for providing information on trends in crime and delinquency. The committee became a catalyst for stimulating the work of other local agencies and co-ordinating the efforts of voluntary bodies with that of the public sector. Where the interests of a particular target group are in conflict with those of the agencies involved, the committee has the task of identifying common ground and constructing a working consensus through a process of consultation and compromise. In practice there is some dispute as to whether such a consensus exists. Jensen (1988) reports that imposed solutions are carefully avoided, but according to Koch (1988), since neither young people nor their parents are represented on SSP committees, initiatives cannot truly represent the interests of the community. Koch (1988) also points out the ambivalent position of police officers - social workers or educationalists one minute, enforcers of the law the next. Principles of trust and confidence, important requirements of effective youth work, can conflict with principles of law enforcement and punishment.

1.6.11   Youth work needs to clarify its position on whether, and if so how, it can contribute to the prevention of crime and criminality. Project drift is likely to occur if youth workers are ambivalent about their role in responding to offending by young people. Youth workers are, understandably, wary of becoming an extended arm of the law, since the effectiveness of their work with young people is largely dependent upon them being able to build up and maintain their trust and confidence. Although youth workers do work directly with young offenders and with representatives of the criminal justice system, it is important that the boundaries between police work and youth work are clearly defined and a code of practice is agreed which clearly sets out how they should work with one another. The police must recognise the youth worker's need to maintain the confidence and trust of young people and similarly, youth workers must respect the importance of the law. The emphasis of youth work should be on preventing young people from becoming offenders rather than helping the police to identify and bring to justice those who have offended. In reaching some understanding with the police about their response to offending by their clients, youth workers may prefer to agree to act as advocates rather than intermediaries.

MULTI-AGENCY YOUTH WORK, WOLVERHAMPTON, ENGLAND

Concern at the extent of youth unemployment in Wolverhampton led to the City Council commissioning a comprehensive study of the social conditions of young people and how local services could best respond to their needs and problems. The subsequent report laid the foundation for the development of policies and strategies for meeting young people's needs. Based on the principle that no single local department or agency can adequately respond to the needs of young people, the main strategy to emerge was the development of an integrated, multi-agency approach for meeting the needs of, and resolving the problems faced by the young.

MULTI-AGENCY YOUTH WORK, WOLVERHAMPTON, ENGLAND (continued)

The City Council was subsequently awarded a grant by the Government for the funding of a five-year project to promote social responsibility amongst the young. To accomplish this, a range of specific strategies were identified, including:

- the identification of peer group networks and patterns of behaviour;

- the identification, with the co-operation of the young people themselves, of situations which lead to crime;

- the exploration of the relationship between these patterns, individual needs and identities and the delinquent activities;

- the provision of alternative sources of prestige and status, and diversion from crime-prone situations into self-chosen activities;

Four detached youth workers were employed (two white females and two Afro-Caribbean males) in two different neighbourhoods - an inner city high rise housing estate and a suburban low rise public (and ex-public) housing estate. Throughout, the scheme emphasised the importance of increasing the extent to which young people take responsibility for choosing and to a large extent managing their own activities within the community. Youth workers were expected to identify and work with natural peer groups at risk and keep in close contact with local schools, parents and a range of community and other agencies, including the police. In some instances, they acted as intermediaries between the police and the local youth and advocated on behalf of some of the young people known to them who had to appear in court.

The principle objective of diverting young people away from crime through detached youth work changed substantially during the five-year period of funding. The initial concern with reducing crime was gradually replaced by work with girls and the promotion of equal opportunities. Ultimately, what started out as an innovative and imaginative departure from mainstream youth work came increasingly to resemble more traditional forms of youth work, reflecting local and national youth work priorities.

The project suffered from a lack of management support, poor planning and little direction. An inter-agency network was established, but in practice it was largely ineffective. A lack of professional status and the power which accompanies statutory responsibilities hindered the ability of youth workers to engage other agencies and be seen as an equal partner in inter-agency forums. This in turn limited their capacity to advocate on behalf of those young people at risk who fall through the net of mainstream agency provision. There was little evidence of successful attempts to change the social and economic conditions of young people through improving their access to agency provision, although project participants valued the relationships they built up with project workers and strong relationships were forged with some young people at risk of offending, including those beyond the reach of other agencies (e.g. those permanently excluded from school) (Smith, 1994).

MULTI-AGENCY YOUTH WORK, WOLVERHAMPTON, ENGLAND (continued)

Despite these limitations, project users reported lower levels of offending (with the exception of older white males) than non-users over the duration of the project, although it had the least effect on the most delinquent. Evident changes in behaviour tended to be moderate and temporary, rather than substantial and permanent. A tension was noted between working with a few at risk individuals on an intensive basis or with more individuals in a less concentrated and more diffuse way. The former is unlikely to have any impact on local levels of crime, whilst the latter is unlikely to have a sustained impact over time.

1.6.12   As with all interventions with young people at risk, care must be taken to avoid labelling and net-widening. The former may occur when relatively minor misbehaviour is re-defined as problematic behaviour requiring official intervention. Care must therefore be taken to ensure that the targeting of resources on offenders does not inadvertently broaden to include youngsters who are not criminal but, for example, come from criminogenic backgrounds or associate with offenders.

1.6.13   To avoid net-widening and the negative consequences of singling out and stigmatising young people, whilst ensuring that those most in need of resources actually receive them, is a difficult task. One way of resolving this is to target people in groups in the areas in which they live rather than as individuals. Resources should be primarily targeted to areas with low provision of services, high crime and high unemployment, and during specific periods when levels of supervision are low, such as after school and during the school holidays. In addition, care should be taken to ensure that those groups most in need of resources, such as migrants, ethnic minorities, the socially and econom- ically disadvantaged, should have easy access to these resources. In some cases, it may also be appropriate to target specific youth-related problems, such as drug-addiction, prostitution and youth homelessness.

1.6.14   Notwithstanding the limitations of youth work in preventing criminality, there are at least five ways in which youth workers, in collaboration with young people, can make a contribution to the prevention of crime and criminality. They can: (i) identify peer group networks and patterns of behaviour which lead to conflicts and offending; (ii) explore the relationships between these patterns and situations and the individual and collective needs and identities of the young people concerned; (iii) seek to encourage alternative sources of acquiring self-esteem, prestige and status; (iv) facilitate access to the services of local agencies; and (v) supervise young people on the streets and seek to divert them from crime-prone situations into legitimate, self- chosen activities.

1.7   EMPLOYMENT POLICY

1.7.1   The relationship between employment and crime is highly complex. The effects of unemployment on crime have not so far been successfully isolated from a wide range of other socio-economic factors, such as income distribution and inequality, urban deprivation and deficits in education (see Tarling, 1982; Box, 1987; Bellknap, 1989). What evidence there is suggests that the relationship between unemployment rates and crime rates is equivocal. However, at the individual level, particularly amongst young males, there is some evidence to suggest that boys are more likely to commit offences, particularly property offences, during periods of unemployment (Farrington, et al. 1986).

1.7.2   There are a number of reasons why unemployment could lead to crime, from lack of income to boredom, demoralisation and the de-stabilisation of the family unit. It is known that unemployment can precipitate family break-up and that this in turn may increase the vulnerability of children within the family to become delinquent (Lenkowski, 1987). It is also known that criminals are more likely to be unemployed than non-offenders (Association of Chief Officers of Probation, 1993) and that unemployed youth are more likely than those in work to hang around the streets and seek or succumb to opportunities to commit offences (Rutter and Giller, 1983). On balance, therefore, it would appear that while there is little evidence to support a causal relationship between unemployment and crime, they are likely to reinforce one another.

1.7.3   Where economic changes lead to increases in migration, unemployment and social disorganisation, increases in crime may well follow. And the more an area or community is socially disorganised, the more vulnerable it is to economic changes (McGahey, 1986). This suggests that different neighbourhoods will be more or less likely to experience increases in crime as a result of changes in economic circumstances, including increases in unemployment. The negative effects of economic changes in general and increases in unemployment rates in particular, will also tend to fall disproportionately on those least able to protect themselves from such changes - the economically and socially disadvantaged and in particular those suffering from severe multiple deprivation.

1.7.4   Generally, employment and training programmes set up with the explicit purpose of reducing crime are few and far between and even those which have had a crime preventive objective have been largely ineffective (McGahey, 1986). In a meta-analysis of 63 employment programmes, Hawkins and Lishner (1983) nevertheless identified a number of common elements in employment programmes which show promise for preventing criminality:

  * job satisfaction and positive feedback on performance;

  * opportunities for promotion and advancement;

  * rapport with supervisors and co-workers;

  * opportunities to use one's skills and learn new skills;

  * status and incremental rewards;

1.7.5   Projects which have physically and socially removed participants from high crime neighbourhoods and crime prone peer groups (in contrast to those which have to work within the participant's natural environment), have proved to be quite effective in reducing propensities to offend in the removed group (Taggart, 1981). However, such programmes are somewhat artificial and of little benefit if participants are ultimately returned to their original areas of residence.

1.7.6   Detailed descriptions of successful employment and training initiatives are rare (although the ete-jeunes project described earlier could reduce the risk of increases in juvenile crime during the summer holidays, when the rate of unemployment is swelled by the new wave of school leavers). This section, more than others, therefore relies more on general accounts of policy initiatives in the field of employment and training development, such as the U.S. Department of Justice's report on employment-based strategies for delinquency prevention (Beville and Nickerson, 1981).

1.7.7   Employment programmes which focus on providing long-term, quality employment are more likely to be effective than those which attempt to change attitudes and behaviour or only provide short-term employment. According to Beville and Nickerson (1981), employment is only likely to reduce delinquency if it provides a sense of commitment, attachment and belief. The employee should be suitably equipped to do the job, both in terms of ability and training, be assisted in the development of good relationships with other employees and learn the rules and standards which govern the running of the organisation or enterprise.

1.7.8   More specifically, there are three main kinds of employment-based approaches which may help to reduce or prevent crime: (i) the provision of training and work experience; (ii) improving and expanding employment opportunities; and (iii) supporting and encouraging employment networks.

(I)   TRAINING AND WORK EXPERIENCE

1.7.8.1 Without educational or vocational qualifications, young people will have lower prospects of securing stable, full-time employment irrespective of the level of available opportunities. Unqualified school leavers who are unable to obtain employment may be particularly vulnerable to the attractions of criminal activities. The existence of large numbers of unemployed young men has been linked to an increase in the growth of single parent families (Wilson, 1987) and to an undermining of the work-related aspirations of school children (Bright, 1992). Programmes which facilitate a successful transition from school to work by preparing school leavers for entering the job market or apprenticeship schemes and expanding educational opportunities outside the school system need to be combined with remedial and support programmes for those who fail or drop out of school. Equally, vocational and employment training programmes which combine on-the-job training with further education and preparation for employment need to be increasingly geared to the rapidly changing employment needs of industry.

1.7.8.2 An exemplary system of employment training exists in Germany where approximately 70 per cent of young people entering the job market do so through an apprenticeship (Currie, 1993). Young people are taught about specific jobs at an early age and on leaving school many sign training contracts with future employers which combine on-the-job training with further part-time schooling. The German training scheme is managed by a quasi-public agency with representatives from business, government and the unions and successful trainees are virtually guaranteed employment on completion of their apprenticeship.

1.7.8.3 Training and retraining should be linked to the requirements of the local market in general and local employers in particular, taking into account changes in patterns of employment, technological developments and career aspirations. Along with work experience, it should provide formal qualifications in technical and vocational skills, courses in life-skills and community service and, if necessary, remedial courses in areas such as literacy and numeracy. It should also focus on improving the readiness of individuals for the disciplines of the world of work, with its specific rules and expectations. Some, particularly those who have been unemployed for a prolonged period and those who have never had the opportunity to work, may need on-the-job training, gradual exposure to work and various forms of social support. To enhance their employability, subsidies can be offered to local businesses in exchange for employment guarantees.

1.7.8.4 Special sheltered groups can be formed consisting of about ten trainees, who are either at risk of offending or who have offended. Each group has its own leader, preferably a mature, experienced, socially adept employee with the ability to empathise and earn the respect of the group. They are responsible for setting group standards of performance and behaviour and developing levels of motivation and conformity to the requirements of a normal working environment. The group then acts as a mechanism for instilling a sense of work discipline and gradually socialising members into the role of a full-time employee.

1.7.8.5 Temporary placement strategies can also be used to effectively fit trainees to jobs and indeed vice versa. Where only short-term, unskilled work is available, strategies for placing trainees in long-term, semi-skilled or skilled work with prospects should be developed. Ultimately, however, resources for training and work experience will be largely wasted without the development of employment opportunities.

(II) IMPROVING AND EXPANDING EMPLOYMENT OPPORTUNITIES

1.7.8.6 In so far as crime represents a rational response to limited or blocked opportunities, creating jobs and providing opportunities for advancement in existing jobs may help to reduce crime. Newly created jobs should be directed towards long-term employment rather than be just stop-gaps, which may hardly differ from employees' experience to date and to which crime is more likely to represent an attractive alternative. Where possible, the creation of new employment opportunities should be based on developing the local economy.

New employment opportunities should benefit the local community, since this is more likely to produce further employment opportunities which coincide with the needs and skills of local residents. Where skills are not available locally, it may be necessary to ensure those most at risk are offered skills training before employment development plans are implemented to ensure new companies resist bringing labour with them or recruiting from outside.

1.7.8.7   Often the health of local economies are heavily reliant on influences outside their control, including macro-economic policies and national trends in unemployment and economic growth. The relationship between national and local economies is highly complex, but where possible, attempts should be made to link and rationalise employment policies at different levels, even though this may be very difficult to achieve in practice. Similarly, some co-operation between the public and private sectors can help to maximise employment opportunities by, for example, offering specific incentives, including financial incentives, such as those used to persuade organisations to employ ex-offenders or relocate in areas of economic decline.

1.7.8.8   In addition to the quantity of employment opportunities, the quality of existing employment should be enhanced so as to provide a greater incentive to apply for and keep jobs. As well as income, work should also provide a degree of satisfaction, a source of identity and status and long-term prospects. A pleasant working atmosphere, a degree of independence, opportunities to learn and positive feedback can all help employees to feel committed to and involved in their work, and ultimately less disposed towards crime.

MISSION LOCALES, FRANCE

Mission Locales are youth training centres which provide a place for young people aged 16 to 25 to meet, discuss and resolve problems associated with employment, training, finance and, in some cases, accommodation with professional experts. Many of the clients are unemployed and/or unqualified school leavers. The Mission uses its local contacts to help to find places on training schemes and it offers courses in literacy and numeracy and advice on applying for temporary and permanent employment.

An important principle of the Mission Locales is to help young people develop projects themselves. Grants are available for starting up enterprises and any young people, provided they are not in employment, can propose a project and apply for funding with the help of the Mission staff. Projects are discussed informally by a special committee, which will also try to make constructive suggestions for improvements and potential sources of finance. Once approved by the committee, the project will then be submitted to the local crime prevention council (CCPD) with a recommendation for partial or full financing (King, 1988). Projects such as a multi-racial theatre workshop, dance parties, sports clubs and camping and study holidays have been funded.

> ## MISSION LOCALES, FRANCE (continued)
>
> Mission Locales are locally based, with contacts to professional workers and employers and its own broadly based management committee. The latter includes among its membership local representatives from trade unions, government departments, trade councils and the voluntary sector. Half of the funding is generated locally, the other half comes from central government. However, while large numbers of young people use the services offered by Mission Locales and many employment and training places are created each year, it is not known what influence this has had on crime, whether at the individual or the community-wide level.

(III) SUPPORTING AND ENCOURAGING EMPLOYMENT NETWORKS

1.7.8.9   In addition to providing adequate training and employment opportunities, networks providing basic information on the types of jobs available and the requirements for and daily content of different jobs should be developed. In addition to such formal networks, informal networks, which facilitate the procurement of jobs via personal contact with friends and relatives, can also be supported and enhanced. A healthy informal employment network is one which is based on a healthy adult employment market, characterised by long term employment prospects in semi-skilled and skilled jobs. The creation of a stable, adult employment market should be the first priority in so far as this provides a sound basis for enhancing employment opportunities for the young.

1.7.8.10 In unstable, socially disorganised communities where economic development is most difficult, the public sector can be used to compensate for a lack of informal networks amongst the most marginalised groups, such as ethnic minorities and migrants. Contract compliance initiatives and the provision of special access centres are two strategies which can help to increase levels of access to employment opportunities for such groups. Detached or outreach youth workers can be used to make contact with and recruit new trainees and employees and employment development workers can be used to co-ordinate the work of other relevant local departments and to link up formal and informal employment markets..

CHAPTER 2. SITUATIONAL CRIME PREVENTION

2.1   INTRODUCTION

2.1.1   Situational crime prevention comprises measures directed at specific forms of crime which involve the management, design or manipulation of the immediate environment in which these crimes occur in as systematic and permanent way as possible, so as to reduce the opportunities for committing these crimes (Hough et al., 1980).

2.1.2   Situational theory is based on the assumption that people choose to commit crime and that the decision to offend is influenced by situational factors. It has been contrasted with what has been referred to as 'dispositional' theory, which gives greater weight to factors operating in the past by which people come to acquire or inherit general dispositions to offend (Clarke, 1980). Situational theory and 'dispositional theory' are not necessarily incompatible and may be viewed instead as applying to different stages in the development of criminal behaviour. Situational crime prevention can also be contrasted with criminality prevention, which tends to focus on offenders rather than offences.

2.1.3   Situational prevention applies most readily to property and other forms of acquisitive crime, such as residential burglary, shoplifting and vandalism, but may also be applicable to other offences, including violent offences under certain circumstances. The attraction of situational measures lies largely in their capacity to provide realistic, often simple and inexpensive solutions to specific kinds of offending in a variety of specific locations. Their success, however, depends upon the extent to which potential offenders perceive situational changes as adversely influencing the ease, the risks and the rewards of committing offences and whether these perceptions affect their decisions as to whether to commit an offence or not. Some situational measures are likely to affect the decision making of potential offenders more than others, whilst certain potential offenders are likely to be influenced more or less by changes in situations than others.

2.1.4   There are three principal kinds of situational measures:

- those which increase the effort of offending;

- those which increase the risks of offending;

- those which reduce the rewards of offending (Clarke, 1992).

Frequently, crime prevention projects draw on a combination of these measures. Examples of multi-measure projects which combine a range of situational measures are presented towards the end of this chapter, followed by a discussion of displacement, which is considered to be the main potential drawback of the situational approach. Since the situational approach to preventing crime has been largely pioneered in the UK, many of the examples used to illustrate specific measures are British.

2.2   MEASURES WHICH INCREASE THE EFFORT OF OFFENDING

2.2.1   There are at least four ways in which increasing the effort of offending reduces criminal opportunities. These are:

(i)   Target hardening, whereby actions are taken to increase the strength of physical barriers close to or at the site of specific targets;

(ii)   Access control, which comprises the restriction of access to specific areas, such as housing estates or shopping centres;

(iii)   Deflecting offenders, which consists of channelling offenders away from potential targets or towards more acceptable outlets;

(iv)   Controlling facilitators, which consists of ensuring that the means for committing certain offences are restricted or made unavailable.

(I)   TARGET HARDENING

2.2.1.1   This well known approach to reducing criminal opportunities simply amounts to increasing the physical security of targets using locks, reinforced and unbreakable materials, immobilising devices and by placing vulnerable objects behind fences, grilles or screens or in safes. While it could be argued that area-level strategies, such as fencing housing estates, represent forms of 'target hardening', the term is more typically applied to protection relating to individual targets or small groups of targets. The most frequently targeted offences which attract various hardening strategies are robberies, burglaries, shoplifting and thefts of and from vehicles. Five strategies are commonly adopted to harden targets or encourage the hardening of targets - security improvements, security surveys, publicity campaigns, building and design codes and insurance incentives.

Security improvements

2.2.1.2   Security devices are commonly employed to protect various kinds of premises from intrusion. Locks, especially on doors, are the most common hardware used. Owners of dwellings under public ownership can be offered grants to improve the security of their houses or, alternatively, security improvements can be made a condition of grants for general property improvements.

2.2.1.3   Research on the effectiveness of security devices is still relatively sparse and has so far focused predominantly on the offences of burglary and vehicle crime. With respect to household burglaries, research suggests that victims of burglary tend to have lower levels of security than non-victims (Mayhew et al, 1993) and that offenders are more likely to fail to gain entry (and thus carry out a burglary) in households with three or more security measures compared with households with no security measures fitted. Bennett and Wright (1984) also found in interviews with convicted burglars that about one in three said that they would be deterred by special security locks. However, evaluations of burglary prevention projects have shown that those few projects which have relied solely on using security devices have been only qualified successes.

SCOTSWOOD ESTATE, ENGLAND

The Scotswood Estate project involved upgrading the level of security for an entire council-owned housing estate over a relatively short period of time (during the Spring of 1980). The aim of the project was to secure all ground floor points of entry by fitting additional security locks. The effect of the scheme was evaluated using police recorded crime trends over a five-year period spanning the project and public surveys before and after the installation of the additional locks.

The results of the study showed that in the year following the installation of the devices residential burglary on the state increased by nine per cent compared with an increase of 77 per cent in the control area. The evaluation concluded that the security devices had contained burglary on the target estate. However, it was also found that burglary had increased by even greater amounts in two selected displacement areas (86 per cent in one and 98 per cent in the other). Using the rate of change in the control area as an indication of underlying changes in crime rates, the evaluation concluded that the displacement effect accounted for approximately nine per cent of the increase in crime in the first displacement area and 21 per cent in the second displacement area. However, overall, it was concluded that the additional security locks had some effect in containing burglary levels on the estate, that not all crimes prevented on the target estate were displaced to the two displacement areas and that overall there was a net reduction in the number of crimes committed.

2.2.1.4 The introduction of steering column locks on all vehicles (i.e. both new and used) led to immediate and long term reductions in thefts and unauthorised taking of vehicles in Germany. However, this success was offset by a sharp increase in the theft of motor cycles and mopeds which, although also protected by similar locks, were nevertheless more vulnerable (Webb, 1994). In Britain, the introduction of steering column locks to new cars only led to some decline in the theft of new cars, but this was more than offset by increases in thefts of used cars and a displacement effect to thefts from vehicles (Webb, 1994). Whilst more expensive, the comprehensive approach adopted in Germany is likely to be cost-effective in the long term. This suggests that the greatest effect of security on crime is likely to occur when a whole class of potential targets are simultaneously protected.

2.2.1.5 Vandalism to and thefts from public telephone kiosks have been reduced by, for example, replacing aluminium coin boxes with steel ones (Mayhew et al, 1980) and the introduction of protective screens has been found to reduce robberies in post offices (Ekblom, 1987) and other retail banking and finance outlets (Austin, 1988).

ANTI-BANDIT SCREENS, ENGLAND

Between October 1981 and March 1985, the counter screen barrier protection in virtually all of the 1,300 sub-post offices in the London Postal Region was upgraded to give a higher degree of resistance to physical attack. The number of robberies of sub-post offices reduced from 266 in 1981 (the year of the start of the initiative) to 121 in 1985. During this period, however, there were more general reductions in robbery rates involving business premises in the Metropolitan Police District. In order to separate the effect of the security initiative from other background effects, three estimates of likely background changes in robbery over the same period were generated. All three estimates suggested some evidence of a security effect associated with the installation of the anti-bandit screens, which ranged from 65 per cent fewer successful offences to 10 per cent fewer successful offences. The overall conclusion was that anti-bandit screens had probably reduced robberies against sub-post offices by about one-third of the expected level over the 22 month follow-up period.

Security surveys

2.2.1.6   Security surveys comprise an assessment of the security needs of specific buildings and in particular the identification of deficiencies and the determination of requirements within a given level of risk. They may be undertaken by specialised police officers or others, such as insurance companies and community crime prevention agencies, who should tailor their advice to the security needs of individual property owners. Fennelly (1982) provides a detailed checklist of nearly 200 items which security surveys should assess. The evidence, however, suggests that in practice very few households request such surveys and that the scope for reducing burglaries in this way is limited by the difficulties associated with persuading people to take up the advice offered (Laycock, 1989). There is also some evidence to suggest that burglary victims in receipt of security surveys become more fearful of crime than those who do not (Rosenbaum, 1988). Nevertheless, there is some evidence that residents who comply with the recommendations of security surveys are less likely to be victimised (ITREC, 1977).

Publicity campaigns

2.2.1.7   People can be encouraged to install security devices or improve their security behaviour through publicity campaigns. Because certain crimes, such as thefts from homes and cars, are widespread and many of these crimes are facilitated by the negligence of owners, publicity campaigns aimed at raising the awareness of potential victims to guard against such crimes have become commonplace. However the effects of such campaigns, whether conducted through radio, television broadcasts, advertising in the press or the distribution of leaflets, are difficult to measure. It appears that while they may increase levels of knowledge and concern, they are less effective in changing security behaviour or reducing crime rates, except perhaps in the short term (Mayhew, 1984) or if highly localised (Laycock, 1991). In the USA, the 'Take A Bite Out of Crime' public information campaign, which features a dog called McGruff as a cartoon character, was evaluated in two stages in 1979 and 1981.

'TAKE A BITE OUT OF CRIME', USA

The first stage of the evaluation comprised a national survey of 1,200 adults and the second stage a panel survey of adults in three cities. The national survey found that about half of the sample saw the advertisements, about a quarter said they had taken precautions and about the same proportion said they felt more fearful of victimisation than before. There was also no evidence of improvements of perceptions of neighbourhood crime or a sense of safety at night.

The surveys showed that the positive effects of the campaign were unevenly distributed among the population investigated. More affluent respondents tended to take precautions which involved co-operation with others, whereas less affluent respondents tended to take more individualistic precautions, such as installing security lighting. Similarly, women tended to favour co-operative activities, whereas men tended to favour individualistic measures, such as buying a guard dog. The evaluation concluded that the programme had affected security behaviour amongst a substantial minority, but had either no effect or an adverse effect on fear of crime and the perceived risk of victimisation (O'Keefe and Mendelsohn, 1984).

2.2.1.8   Thus care needs to be taken in the planning of publicity campaigns to ensure that they do not inadvertently increase fear of crime and/or lead to over-reaction. Where combined with other measures, such as increases in police patrols, publicity campaigns may be more likely to increase the willingness of householders and vehicle owners to take precautions without becoming more fearful of being victimised.

PUBLICITY CAMPAIGNS IN THE NETHERLANDS

Three projects in the Netherlands which combine publicity campaigns with other measures, have recorded some successes. The projects - in The Hague, Amsterdam and Hoogeveen - combined the provision of information and advice and increases in police foot and bicycle patrols with traditional investigative functions. The three project areas, each matched with control areas, produced different results, but all three resulted in an increased willingness of residents to take precautions. The project in The Hague resulted in a short term drop in burglary rates which, according to van Dijk and Steinmetz (1981), was not due to more widespread use of precautionary measures or patrols, but to the publicity campaign. Interestingly, the burglary rate began to increase after the project disbanded. The other two projects did not result in a decline in burglaries, but since burglaries increased elsewhere, this can be considered a limited success.

Building and design codes

2.2.1.9   A more comprehensive approach to protecting dwellings from burglary might be developed by ensuring that new buildings, and even entire areas, comply with specific security standards. National codes detailing the costs of installing different levels of security in various kinds of properties and guidelines for architects and builders on building security have been developed in some countries. For example, a working group on residential burglary in Britain made recommendations with respect to local authority housing investment programmes in high risk areas (Standing Conference on Crime Prevention, 1986). The report provided information on the costs of installing different levels of security in properties with various kinds of doors and windows and recommended that care should be taken to ensure that crime preventive measures would not conflict with fire-prevention and other safety requirements.

2.2.1.10 There are few evaluations of the effectiveness of building codes. One study which has examined the effect of building codes on burglary was conducted on the Hillfield Estate in Bristol (Poyner and Webb, 1987).

BUILDING SECURITY GUIDELINES, ENGLAND

In 1981, specifications for residential security levels were drawn up by an Architectural Liaison Officer in response to an expressed concern by tenants that the condition of the houses on the estate was deteriorating. The specifications were similar to British Standard guidelines on the security of dwellings which recommended levels of security which would withstand a determined attempt to break in. An analysis of police recorded crime over a period of years before and after the improvements showed that burglaries among the 750 improved houses remained stable and low (less than 10 burglaries a year over the years following the improvements), while burglaries in the surrounding beat area as a whole almost doubled. The evaluation concluded that the small number of offences involved made it difficult to draw any firm conclusions. However, they believed that the evaluation showed that the area was protected from the more general growth in crime in the surrounding district.

2.2.1.11 Developments in technology have produced more sophisticated ways of hardening targets. Southall and Ekblom (1985), for example, considered the feasibility of reducing thefts of, and from, cars through the introduction of a range of mechanical and electronic security devices at the design stage. In addition to steering column locks, they suggested that the 'crime-free car' should have central locking, an alarm, windows made of reinforced glass and registration numbers etched on windows to reduce its resaleability if stolen. If possible, security devices should be standardised and builders and manufacturers should be obliged to conform to national minimum security standards. To be successful motor manufacturers need to be persuaded that they are responsible for producing secure vehicles. One way of assisting this is to set up a public index of thievability, which draws attention to vehicles most at risk of being broken into and stolen. Such an index can help to show that crime can be designed out, raise public expectations concerning vehicle security and place greater pressure on vehicle manufacturers to improve the security of their product. Similarly, advertising campaigns which include references to security as well as safety, speed and other aspects of performance, may also help towards reducing auto-related crime. There are now clear signs that motor manufacturers are indeed beginning to take vehicle security at the design stage more seriously.

Insurance incentives

2.2.1.12 The provision of insurance constitutes a potentially influential means through which financial incentives can be offered to promote the adoption of crime prevention measures. By insisting on the installation of security hardware as a condition of providing insurance cover, insurance companies might persuade householders to take-up security measures. Recent figures from eight leading insurance companies in Britain show that companies are typically willing to reduce premiums by between 5 per cent and 10 per cent when approved window and door locks are fitted (Papworth, 1994).

2.2.1.13 It should be noted that providing incentives to householders to improve home security is likely to be less effective in relation to poorer people living in poorer areas. Poorer people are less likely to be able to afford insurance and poor areas are likely to evoke higher premiums because of their relatively greater risk of burglary and household theft. To increase the take up of insurance in such areas, the poorest may need to be subsidised, offered discounts for installing security devices or insured on a block or estate rather than dwelling unit basis. Incentives through the use of no-claims discounts may act as a disincentive to report minor thefts and burglaries and should therefore be avoided. There is as yet little evidence on the effects of commercial insurance on the prevention of crime, although Litton and Pease (1984) suggest that the impact is likely to be minimal.

(II)   ACCESS CONTROL

2.2.2.1   Some crimes can be prevented simply by removing access to a specific target or to whole areas. An example of the former is the widespread replacement of cash with cheques, credit cards and other forms of 'plastic' money to reduce opportunities for crimes such as security van robberies and thefts from telephone kiosks and introducing pre-paid tickets on public transport systems to prevent robberies of takings on trams and buses. The installation of entry-phone systems on housing estates, a common form of access control, has however not proved successful in reducing crime in high-crime areas (Bright et al, 1985), although small reductions in crime have been reported in schemes which combine entry-phones with the installation of perimeter fencing (Poyner and Webb, 1987).

2.2.2.2   The introduction of automatic ticket machines and electronic ticket barriers which control access to and egress from railway platforms has been found to reduce fare evasion. A study by Clarke (1993) of the effects of a change in the system of ticket issuing and collection on the London Underground railway system found that the percentage of passengers found without valid tickets fell substantially in the year during which the new system became operational. Clarke concluded that the system had cut fare evasions by two-thirds.

2.2.2.3   Examples of area wide access control include limiting access to whole neighbourhoods by putting up fencing around and within housing estates, installing road gates or routing roads and footpaths. A recent study in Canada on the influence of street layout on the patterning of property offences suggests that the location of property crime is affected by road access (Beavon et al., 1994). Street segments with just two road turnings leading into it experienced approximately one quarter of the average amount of property crime as street segments with six road turnings leading into it. However, the effectiveness of road barriers in controlling crime will depend on a number of other factors, including whether offenders travel by vehicle or on foot, whether they live near to the area or far away and whether or not the area is a high or low crime area. The use of street closures to reduce prostitution and associated crime in residential areas has also been successful when combined with periods of intensive policing prior to and following the implementation of road closures (Matthews, 1992).

(III)   DEFLECTING OFFENDERS

2.2.3.1   Closely allied to access control, deflecting offenders can include channelling offenders away from potential targets (by introducing traffic flow controls, for example). Clarke (1993) notes that deflecting soccer supporters away from rival teams at the point of entry and within the stadium can reduce the opportunities for assault and that late-night buses can be used to deflect young people out of city centre entertainment areas, where opportunities for crime are high.

HARTFORD NEIGHBOURHOOD CRIME PREVENTION PROGRAMME, USA

The Hartford Neighbourhood Crime Prevention Program included a number of measures, including environmental changes designed to affect vehicle and pedestrian flows. The goals of the physical design part of the programme were to reduce the movement of non-residents through the experimental area. This was achieved by blocking roads and by converting roads to one-way traffic only. The outcome of the design changes was to reduce the movement of vehicles to a single street running north to south and another street running east to west. These design changes were intended to reduce the number of outsiders using the area as a through route either in a vehicle or on foot. An evaluation of the impact of the programme as a whole (including design changes to re-route vehicles and pedestrians) showed a reduction in burglary and street robbery rates over the period of the programme. The researchers attributed at least some of this reduction to the design changes which channelled the movement of outsiders to the area (Fowler, et al., 1979).

2.2.3.2   Additionally, deflecting offenders refers to the channelling of offender motivation to more acceptable outlets. Clarke (1992) provides a number of examples of how this might be achieved, including the use of 'graffiti boards', litter bins, and the provision of public urinals. It is also possible to deflect offenders away from high and towards low victimisation targets, for example by tolerating prostitution in specific 'red-light' districts, or certain areas of city centres, in order to contain the problem more easily.

(IV)   CONTROLLING FACILITATORS

2.2.4.1 Certain types of offences can be prevented if the means for committing them are made unavailable. Screening airline passengers for weapons and explosive devices has reduced the incidence of aircraft 'skyjacking' (Hough et al., 1980) and the potential for violence in pubs and sports stadia has been reduced by replacing beer glasses with plastic containers. The potential for football violence can also be reduced through the systematic searching of football fans prior to matches and the removal of bricks, stones and other potential weapons around football grounds. Suicides through inhaling toxic domestic gas and the fumes of car exhausts have also been reduced by replacing toxic with non-toxic substances (Clarke and Mayhew, 1988; Lester, 1993).

2.2.4.2 One of the most widely discussed potential facilitators of violent crime is the availability of hand guns and other firearms. Attempts to estimate the relationship between gun availability and violent crime tend to show that there is some correlation between the two (Cook, 1982; Wright et al., 1983; Lester, 1993). However, despite these correlations, there is no conclusive evidence which shows a direct causal link between gun availability and crime. A central problem associated with determining the relationship between gun availability and violent crime is that there are, at least in the USA, no direct measures of gun availability. Nevertheless Rosenbaum (1988), referring to the situation in the USA, states that:

> "...an estimated 30,000 deaths occur each year because of criminal, accidental or suicidal uses of firearms; in another 900,000 incidents firearms are present, fired, or involved in some other capacity. One cannot help asking what the overall picture might be if the opportunities for using firearms were curtailed dramatically."

2.3   MEASURES WHICH INCREASE THE RISKS OF OFFENDING

2.3.1   The risks of offending are increased if the real or perceived threat of detection, apprehension and/or conviction can be increased. Thus attaching electronic tags to retail goods, detector strips to library books or applying olfactory chemicals to carpets may all help to deter or detect offenders. The real or perceived threat of apprehension can also be increased by introducing, or raising the degree of, various forms surveillance. (In contrast to other forms of situational crime prevention, surveillance can be 'person' rather than 'capital' intensive and may therefore be particularly attractive to developing countries). There are three main forms of surveillance:

- formal surveillance, which comprises the defence of property and the detection and deterrence of offenders by people specifically employed to do so, such as the police, security guards and store detectives;

- surveillance by employees, which differs from formal surveillance only in that it is carried out by people employed
primarily for other purposes, such as the caretakers of
residential and other kinds of premises;

- natural surveillance, which consists of the protection of
people and property afforded by the capacity of ordinary
citizens to exercise a degree of surveillance as they go about
their everyday activities.

(I)   FORMAL SURVEILLANCE

2.3.1.1   The group most frequently associated with formal surveillance is the
police. The police have the specific role of apprehending and deterring
potential offenders and, in the early days of the police, formal surveillance
through simple patrolling was regarded as their primary function. Until the
early 1970s it was widely believed that police patrols were fairly effective in
achieving this objective, but since then the effectiveness of the police in
deterring and detecting crime has been questioned by the findings of a number
of research and evaluation studies. The best known of these was the Kansas
City Preventive Patrol Experiment (Kelling et al., 1974) which investigated the
effect of changing the number of vehicle patrols.

THE KANSAS CITY PREVENTIVE PATROL EXPERIMENT, USA

In five reactive beats routine preventive vehicle patrol was eliminated and
officers were instructed to respond only to calls for service. In five control
beats routine preventive vehicle patrol was maintained at its usual level of
one car per beat. In the remaining five proactive beats routine vehicle
preventive patrol was intensified by two to three times its usual level
through the assignment of additional patrol cars. The beats were allocated to
each of the research conditions by random assignment. The results of pre-
test and post-test victimisation surveys showed that the experimental patrols
had no significant effect on any of the categories of crime investigated.
There was also no change in reporting rates to the police, citizens attitudes
to the police, in public satisfaction with the police service, in security
behaviour among residents, or in fear of crime, or in police response times.
The Kansas City experiment has since been criticised on the grounds that
the small sample sizes used lacked statistical power and on the grounds that
the programme was not implemented as intended (Larson, 1976). However,
the results had considerable impact on beliefs about the effectiveness of
police patrol.

2.3.1.2   Vehicle patrols have the added disadvantage of tending to emphasise the
law enforcement aspects of policing at the expense of the community relations or
peace keeping aspects (Kelling et al. 1974). Some even argue that vehicle patrols
increase crime in so far as committing resources to such patrols (and indeed
other kinds of reactive work) means less resources for preventive work, which
leads to more crime and disorder, which increases public demand for more
vehicle patrols and other forms of reactive policing (Beckett and Hart, 1981).

2.3.1.3 Since the Kansas City evaluation there have been a large number of studies which have tested the effect of police presence on crime. These studies can be split into two groups. The first group comprises experiments which involve variations in the number of routine foot (or vehicle) patrols covering beat or normal policing areas. Research suggests that increases in police manpower in general do not necessarily lead to reductions in crime or clear up rates and may even lead to increases, at least in recorded crime (see, for example, Clarke and Hough, 1984). However, an evaluation of the implementation of foot patrols in Michigan, USA showed an overall reduction in crime in the year following the introduction of foot patrols in 14 neighbourhoods compared with the year before (Trojanowicz, 1986). On the whole, the findings of research on the effects of increasing the number of foot patrol officers are equivocal, although since the chances of actually being present at the scene of a crime are very remote (Clarke and Hough, 1984), it seems unlikely that increasing the number of patrols will influence crime levels directly.

2.3.1.4 The second group comprises experiments which involve increases in the density of foot (or vehicle) patrols for specific periods of time and in specific locations. These experiments have tended to produce more positive findings. In Minneapolis in the USA, patrol officers were instructed to visit 55 randomly assigned crime 'hot spots' during the time when they were not responding to calls for service. In comparison with a further 55 'hot spots', where the police continued their normal patrol operations, levels of crime and calls for assistance were found to be lower in the experimental areas. Furthermore, the rate of disorder was significantly lower during periods of police presence at the 'hot spot' than during the period of police absence (Koper et al., 1992; Sherman and Weisburd, 1992).

2.3.1.5 Experiments in which the police change what they do while on patrol have also led to reductions in crime. A study by Boydstun (1975) on the effect of field interrogations (police stops) showed that the suspension of field interrogation was associated with an increase in crime and the resumption of field interrogation was associated with a reduction in crime.

2.3.1.6 In addition to the work of the public police, formal surveillance is provided by a wide range of privately employed groups of guards, supervisors and patrols. The private security industry has expanded considerably over the last 10 years in North America and Europe. Recent estimates in Britain, for example, suggest that the size of the private security industry now exceeds the size of the public police service (Campbell and Travis, 1994). Traditionally, the services of private security companies have been commonly employed in the commercial sector. In recent years, security firms have become active in semi-public premises, such as shopping centres, airports and holiday complexes and in some countries police forces have entered into partnerships with private security firms.

2.3.1.7 The expansion of the size and scope of surveillance by the private security industry raises questions about their authority and their relationship with the police. The activities of private security officers may need to be regulated by legislation. Common elements are requirements for the screening and training of security personnel and arrangements for supervision by the police.

2.3.1.8   One of the fastest areas of expansion has been in the area of residential neighbourhood patrols. According to a recent survey, private residential street patrols either operate, or are about to begin operating, in almost half of the police force areas in England and Wales (The Times, 15 March, 1994). Such patrols have a longer history in the USA and parts of Eastern Europe. So far, the effectiveness of private police operations has not been fully evaluated, although a study of the effect of a number of interventions on shoplifting from retail outlets found that the presence of security guards had no significant effect on levels of shoplifting (Farrington et al., 1993).

(II)   SURVEILLANCE BY EMPLOYEES

2.3.2.1   Surveillance by employees such as shop assistants, hotel doormen, park keepers, car park attendants, mail and milk delivery personnel, meter readers, taxi drivers, appliance repair personnel, teachers, stewards at sports stadia and train drivers and conductors, can help to prevent or detect crime (Clarke, 1992). In Canada, farmers carry out surveillance duties as part of their daily work, using their own vehicles, including light aircraft, to identify and record suspicious vehicles, persons or incidents. One of the most common form of employee surveillance is by caretakers on housing estates and by concierges at the entrances to high-rise residential blocks and other premises, both of which have been found to reduce levels of vandalism and burglary and increase feelings of safety and social interaction amongst local occupants (Poyner and Webb, 1987).

RECEPTION CENTRE, ENGLAND

An evaluation of the introduction of a reception service into a high-rise public housing block in London, England, found that burglary and attempted burglary rates reduced from a high point of 14 per year to between 3 to 7 per year in the following three years (Poyner and Webb, 1987). When the experimental and control blocks were compared for the time of day when the reception desk was in operation (8-00 a.m. to 11-00 p.m. Mondays to Fridays) the results showed that the experimental block had a larger reduction in burglary and attempted burglary than any of the control blocks. However, the researchers acknowledged that large year-on-year variations in either direction were not uncommon among the blocks.

It was also found that the presence of a receptionist increased feelings of safety, improved levels of social interaction amongst tenants and reduced maintenance costs. Along with the introduction of tenant consultation, these changes probably contributed to the scheme's success in creating a greater sense of community amongst tenants.

2.3.2.3   Sturman (1980) found in England that buses with ticket conductors are less prone to vandalism, and in Canada DesChamps et al. (1991) found that the deployment of additional ticket inspectors during the rush hour periods on the Vancouver Regional Transit System reduced fare evasion. In the Netherlands, a similar experiment which employed ticket inspectors on the tram and bus system provides further evidence of the crime reduction potential of surveillance by employees.

THE VIC. PROJECT, THE NETHERLANDS

In the Netherlands, an experimental project employed over 1,000 young people between the ages of 19 and 28, many of them unemployed, to tackle petty crime on public transport (van Andel, 1989). Following the disappearance of conductors on trams and buses for reasons of economy, the informal supervision carried out by such personnel also disappeared. Consequently, opportunities for fare-dodging and other offences, especially vandalism, increased. The introduction of these teams of young supervisors coincided with a change in boarding procedures such that tickets were checked by the driver before a passenger could enter the vehicle.

The project was implemented in three cities: Amsterdam, Rotterdam and The Hague. The recruits (including both men and women as well as ethnic minority group members) were given short training courses in criminal law and ticket inspection. In Amsterdam, the recruits worked in groups of two to four to operate random checks on trams and buses. Once they had checked a tram or metro train they got out and boarded another. In Rotterdam, the VICs checked trams on a random basis and also provided a permanent presence at the metro stations, at which they provided information and fulfilled a deterrent function. In both Amsterdam and Rotterdam, the VICs were authorised to impose fines. In the Hague, a more 'customer friendly' approach was adopted and VICs travelled in pairs on the trams and were not authorised to impose fines. Passengers caught without a ticket were given the choice of buying one from the driver or getting off the tram.

The results of a before and after evaluation, showed that fare-dodging declined in all three cities. The largest reductions were on the buses which included the new system of ticket checking. The percentage of fare dodges reduced from nine per cent to two per cent in Amsterdam, from four per cent to one per cent in Rotterdam, and from 14 per cent to two per cent in The Hague.

The project did not measurably affect the level of aggression by passengers against tram drivers or the perceptions of safety among passengers. The number of attacks against passengers fell from five per cent in the 'before' survey of passengers to three per cent in the 'after' survey. There was a reduction in the amount of graffiti inside metro stations in Rotterdam, although the amount on external walls remained unchanged. At the same time, the number of windows in bus and tram shelters which needed replacing during the experimental period doubled, which perhaps suggests displacement of vandalism from the stations to the streets.

2.3.2.4 There are a number of technical appliances which can enhance the capacity of individuals to exercise effective surveillance. Closed circuit television (CCTV) may enhance the surveillance function of both dedicated and general employees, whilst alarms may enhance the surveillance function not only of employees, but also formal agencies of control and members of the public. Both CCTV and alarms increase the risks of offending since their primary function is to detect and deter offenders.

CCTV

2.3.2.5   CCTV systems have been installed in a wide variety of settings and evaluations of their effectiveness have also been conducted in a wide range of locations. Mayhew (1984) reports the findings of a study (Musheno et al., 1978) which evaluated a CCTV surveillance system installed in three blocks of flats in New York which showed no reduction in crime following the implementation of the system. A similar study in London, also mentioned by Mayhew (1984), provided more encouraging findings (Smith, 1980).

RESIDENTIAL CCTV SECURITY SYSTEM, ENGLAND

Video cameras were fitted at the entrance to four high rise residential blocks and the output was fed to a caretaker and to the communal television aerial system which enabled all residents in the flat to observe the entrance area. The aim of the scheme was for the residents to check who was calling on them before releasing the door catch. In fact many of the residents 'tuned in' to the video camera channel as it offered 'compelling' viewing. The only concern expressed by residents at a local meeting was that offenders living in the tower blocks would be able to 'tune in' to determine who was leaving the block and then burgle their flats. The offender could turn to the victims' viewing channel to observe when the resident returned. In fact, an evaluation of a pilot scheme showed that burglary dropped to zero during the test period and the number of burglaries remained low during the period when all blocks had TV systems installed.

2.3.2.6   There is also some limited evidence of success from the installation of CCTV cameras on public transport. The installation of video cameras on a sample of buses in the north of England in the middle of the 1980s was associated with a reduction in bus vandalism (Poyner, 1988). The first experimental 'video bus' used two cameras connected to a video recorder in the luggage compartment of the bus. At the end of each run the video bus was checked for damage and if any incidents were discovered they were sought out on the video tapes. School children caught damaging the bus on camera were sought out and the school and their parents were contacted. It was noted that after a few weeks of this procedure damage to the video bus fell almost to zero and no further follow ups were required.

2.3.2.7   Other studies have shown some reductions in crime following the installation of CCTV on public transport systems. Carr and Spring (1993) described the outcome of a 'Travel Safe' programme implemented on the public transport system in Victoria, Australia which included (amongst other things) the installation of CCTV cameras in stations and on trains. The evaluation reported a 42 per cent reduction in crimes against the person during the first two years of the programme. Similar results were obtained in a study by Burrows (1980) of the effect of installing CCTV systems on the London Underground. Burrows found that thefts and robbery at stations with CCTV surveillance fell by a significant amount in the year following installation. Thefts and robberies at stations without CCTV either fell by a much smaller amount or increased. There is also some evidence that installing CCTV systems in public car parks reduces vehicle crime (Tilley, 1993).

Alarms

2.3.2.8 The use of alarms, especially in dwellings, shops, and vehicles, is increasing. The 1992 British Crime Survey (Mayhew, Maung, and Mirrlees-Black, 1993) showed that 13 per cent of householders interviewed owned a burglar alarm, which was almost double the number reported in the 1988 survey. The 1992 survey also found that at the time of the incident fewer victims (8 per cent) owned burglar alarms than non-victims (10 per cent). The research also showed that within households owning a burglar alarm almost half (49 per cent) of incidents reported resulted in the offender failing to gain entry compared with 31 per cent of households with no security measures. These figures suggest therefore that burglar alarms can be effective in reducing but not eliminating the risk of burglary. Similar findings have been reported in Scotland (McAllister, Leitch and Payne, 1993).

2.3.2.9 Research based on interviews with burglars also concludes that burglar alarms may be an effective deterrent (Bennett and Wright, 1984; Cromwell et al., 1991; Wright and Decker, 1994). However, research by Buck and Hakim (1993) found that owners of alarmed houses who had been burgled generally took fewer precautions than owners of alarmed houses who had not been burgled, which suggests that it may be difficult to isolate the effect of burglar alarm ownership from the wide range of other household character-istics which might explain both alarm ownership and burglary risk.

(III)   NATURAL SURVEILLANCE

2.3.3.1 A central concept relating to surveillance is the idea of 'defensible space' developed by Oscar Newman. Newman describes defensible space as comprising the actual or symbolic barriers which define areas of influence which are under the control of residents (Newman, 1972). A central mechanism of Newman's concept of defensible space is the creation of an environment which maximises the potential for natural surveillance.

2.3.3.2 Some areas are naturally endowed with high visibility whilst others, such as those with poor street lighting, pedestrian tunnels and blind alleys, may not be. Offences are less likely to occur if potential offenders believe they are being overlooked and greater surveillance can be achieved by manipulating the environment - the design, location and lay-out of buildings and the spaces around them - in a wide variety of ways (see, for example, Mayhew et al., 1979; Wilson, S. 1980).

2.3.3.3 In order to prevent crime by increasing natural surveillance, premises and their surrounds should be easily overlooked from the street and neighbouring premises; opportunities for concealment near and inside dwellings should be minimised; cul-de-sacs and the careful placing of fences and other barriers should be used to ensure that access to, and escape from an area discourages strangers and land uses should be mixed to encourage "bustling activity", increase the number of "eyes on the street" and generate a feeling of personal security.

2.3.3.4 Natural surveillance can be enhanced by providing more or better street lighting, but whilst street lighting improvements would seem to reduce fear of crime (Tien et al., 1979), the findings of research on the effect of such improvements on levels of crime are inconclusive. Large-scale evaluations conducted in Britain have tended to show that improved lighting does not affect crime rates (see, for example, Atkins et al., 1991), although one study in London shows that improvements in street lighting can reduce crime in small areas over short periods of time.

STREET LIGHTING IMPROVEMENTS, ENGLAND

An early study of the effect of improvements in street lighting on crime was conducted in Edmonton, London (Painter, 1988). The study aimed to evaluate the effect of improved street lighting in the area of a tunnel through a railway embankment which provided a pedestrian access route to a council estate. The improvements were evaluated by conducting interviews with pedestrians using the tunnel immediately before re-lighting and again six weeks after re-lighting. The interviews covered amongst other things fear and victimisation over a period six weeks and 12 months before the interview. A comparison of the period six weeks before the improvements and six weeks after improvements showed that the total number of reported incidents fell from 21 before re-lighting to three after re-lighting.

2.3.3.5 It is perhaps surprising that there is not more evidence of a crime reduction effect from street lighting evaluations. It might be hypothesized that if there were no street lights or very poor street lights that crime would increase. Mayhew (1976) noted that during the emergency power measures adopted between December 1973 and February 1974 when local councils were asked to cut street lighting by 50 per cent, levels of burglary in Brighton, England increased by 100 per cent and thefts from vehicles by 59 per cent (reported in Fleming and Burrows, 1987). It is possible that whether or not improved lighting reduces crime is conditional upon a number of factors which are not taken into account in the published research.

2.3.3.6 According to Bennett and Wright (1984), accumulated research evidence suggests that premises which are perceived to be either occupied or easily overlooked are least likely to be victimised. They suggest that burglary prevention programmes should therefore be based on ways of increasing the extent to which premises look occupied even if they are not, particularly in dormitory residential areas with high proportions of childless families and working adults. The appearance of occupancy can be achieved by leaving a light on inside, or parking a vehicle outside, the premises. Other precautions like cancelling daily deliveries (e.g. newspapers, milk), may also give the impression that the premises are occupied.

2.3.3.7 The effectiveness or otherwise of natural surveillance in preventing crime may also be contingent upon the preparedness of individuals to intervene in the event of witnessing a suspicious incident (and the perceptions of potential offenders). Willingness to intervene is in turn dependent upon whether residents feel involved in their community and whether they feel their environment is worth protecting and feel responsible for it. The relationship between levels of natural surveillance and community stability is discussed in chapter 3 on community crime prevention.

2.4 MEASURES WHICH REDUCE THE REWARDS OF OFFENDING

2.4.1   The rewards of offending can be reduced by decreasing the expected benefits from committing an offence by, for example, reducing the value of what is stolen. There are four principal ways in which this can be accomplished: (i) by physically removing potential targets of crime; (ii) by marking property; (iii) by removing inducements to commit offences; and (iv) by setting rules to restrict and control behaviour.

(I)   TARGET REMOVAL

2.4.1.1 Target removal comprises, for example, the removal of slot machines from public places to prevent them being vandalised or broken into or the payment of staff by non-cash means in order to remove large amounts of cash on business premises. The concept can also be extended to mean the removal of specific parts of a target such as adding mural paintings to large walls in public places to replace (remove) the blank wall which might otherwise invite graffiti or the prevention of thefts from gas and electricity meters by replacing them with billing systems (see Hill, 1986). Other examples of target removal include various attempts to improve cash handling procedures in retail outlets and commercial enterprises by limiting the amount of cash available, posting signs indicating cash limits, utilising time-release or drop safes and training employees to follow strict cash-control policies (Hunter and Jeffery, 1992).

(II)   PROPERTY MARKING

2.4.2.1 The durable or invisible marking of property such as cars, bicycles and valuable household goods, has the potential to reduce its value by making the property easier to identify and thus less marketable and usable. It is by no means a recent phenomenon - cattle have been branded as a method of identifying ownership for a long time. Names, personal identity numbers or postcodes can be engraved on property with special engraving equipment or ultra-violet pens. A novel, but extremely effective variation is the use of dye capsules in night deposit safes and cash dispensers. In the event of a robbery, the dye capsules are activated and the bank notes become valueless. But merely marking property may not alone determine whether the property, if stolen, is recovered or prevented from being resold (Mayhew, 1984) or whether offenders are more likely to be apprehended (Heller et al., 1975). A large study of the effect of an Operation Identification project in a municipality just outside Stockholm City in Sweden also found little evidence of success (Knutsson, 1984).

OPERATION IDENTIFICATION, SWEDEN

A property marking scheme in Sweden, which was evaluated by the Swedish National Council for Crime Prevention, covered about 3,500, mainly detached, houses. The programme involved leafleting, mobile exhibitions, and door-to-door canvassing of local residents, including the loan of property-marking equipment. Over the four-year period of the project, the percentage of dwellings displaying property marking window stickers increased from 13 per cent to almost 30 per cent. Time-series analyses of police recorded burglaries over the period of the evaluation showed that there was no evidence of a programme effect.

2.4.2.2 A study of the effectiveness of property marking in three villages in South Wales resulted in more positive findings (Laycock, 1985).

PROPERTY MARKING IN CAERPHILLY, WALES

Between 70 per cent and 75 per cent of eligible residents in the three villages participated in the scheme and displayed a property marking sticker in their window. The project was evaluated using a twelve month "before and after" survey of police-recorded crime. The results of the survey showed that the number of houses in the scheme area burgled at least once reduced from 5.1 per cent to 3.0 per cent in the year after the introduction of the scheme. A comparison of the rate of burglary 'before' and 'after' among participants in the scheme and non-participants showed a reduction in burglaries among participants, but not among non-participants. However, no goods were recovered, marked or otherwise.

2.4.2.3 The results of the Welsh study are inconsistent with North American and Swedish experience with property marking. Possible reasons for the success of the Welsh scheme include the extraordinarily high 'take-up' rate among respondents and the effect of the high degree of publicity surrounding the programme. It is also possible that the project was successful because of its special characteristics, including the fact that it was carried out in an isolated and close-knit, rural community.

2.4.2.4 Other rural property-marking schemes have also produced positive results. One scheme established in Canada aimed to prevent the theft of farm chemicals from grain elevators.

THE PORTAGE LA PRAIRIE PROJECT, CANADA

In Portage La Prairie in Canada the police, aware of the difficulties of detecting crime in isolated rural areas, have introduced a number of property marking schemes to reduce the number of thefts. One of these schemes involved the application of highly visible paint marks, with stickers announcing they were marked, to all containers of farm chemicals. The police simultaneously provided a publicity campaign to raise public awareness of the property marking campaign and subsequently thefts of farm chemicals were almost wiped out completely (Linden and Minch, 1985). No evidence is available as to whether thefts declined because of the marking of the property, because of the use of stickers or because the scheme was so widely publicised.

2.4.2.5   Other goods, such as Christmas trees, mechanised farming equipment and livestock, have also been subjected to various forms of marking, tagging or branding. Grain can be very inexpensively marked by mixing small pieces of numbered paper in with the grain. However, while positive results have been claimed for these initiatives, the quality of the evaluations used to assess the effectiveness of these schemes have not been sophisticated. Overall, the results of evaluations of property marking schemes are mixed and few attempt to identify whether observed reductions in thefts are partly or wholly offset by displacement to other unmarked goods, other areas or other forms of crime. It is possible that whether or not property marking reduces crime depends on a number of other factors such as the nature of the community covered by the scheme, the level of publicity and the participation rate.

(III)   REMOVING INDUCEMENTS

2.4.3.1   Property marking tends to cover specific items relating to theft, whereas the category of 'removing inducements' aims to cover other items and offences, including inducements to violence and vandalism. Examples of inducements to crime include the wearing of expensive jewellery on the street, metal road signs which make a satisfying 'clang' when shot at and the attractiveness of certain wall surfaces which almost 'invite' graffiti (Clarke, 1992).

2.4.3.2   Signs of deterioration or dilapidation can be powerful inducements to commit acts of vandalism. Broken windows left unrepaired in a building invite further windows to be broken (Wilson and Kelling, 1982) and blocks with open abandoned buildings were found by Spelman (1993) to experience higher crime rates than blocks without open buildings. The effect of dilapidation as an inducement to crime was part of a study conducted by Zimbardo (1973), who argued that in order for a car to be vandalised it must first provide some 'releaser' stimuli to call attention to itself. The following summarises an experiment which aimed to create 'releaser' stimuli and to observe their effect.

AUTO-STRIPPING EXPERIMENT, USA

Zimbardo and a colleague bought a car and left it on a street near the campus of New York University, after removing the licence plates and leaving the boot and bonnet open to provide the necessary 'releaser' signals. Within ten minutes a family of a father, mother and eight-year-old son began stripping parts off the car. At the end of the first 26 hour period, a steady parade of offenders removed the battery, radiator, air cleaner and other car parts. Nine hours later, teenagers began a process of random destruction. In less than three days the car was reduced to a battered hulk.

At the same time, another car was left on the streets of Palo Alto in California near Stamford University campus, also without licence plates and with the bonnet and boot open. The car remained untouched for a week. It was hypothesized that in this area the 'releaser' cues were not sufficient. Zimbardo and his graduate students decided to begin the process of destruction themselves by attacking the car with a sledgehammer. Observers began to join in and take over and by the end of the day the vehicle had been completely destroyed. Zimbardo concluded that releaser cues were important inducements to certain kinds of vandalism and that their effect will be stronger in areas of relative social anonymity.

(IV)   RULE SETTING

2.4.4.1 'Rule setting' concerns the effect of rules on governing and controlling behaviour. Clarke (1992) gives as examples company rules relating to the use of telephones or cash-handling procedures. Such rules can have a crime prevention effect through regulating and controlling the conduct of both employees and the public. Clarke suggests that the mechanisms by which rule setting might be effective include removing ambiguity in what is and what is not acceptable behaviour and reducing the possibility that potential offenders will be able to use excuses, justifications, or other 'techniques of neutralisation' of the kind noted by Matza (1964) to neutralise the moral bind of the law and facilitate offending.

2.4.4.2 A study by Smith and Burrows (1986) drew attention to the need to set clear rules for accounting and stock control procedures in order to reduce losses and fraud. They give an example of a public hospital which consistently failed to balance its catering budget. An investigation revealed that there were a number of vulnerable points in its accounting and stock control procedures including: Saturday morning deliveries, which were unsupervised; stocks held in hospital wards, which were largely unmonitored; and orders made for stock from the central supplies, which were not systematically recorded. The discovery of a long-standing fraud involving people of responsibility in the hospital led to various changes to the operating procedure which led to a reduction in the annual deficit.

2.5   MULTIPLE MEASURE SITUATIONAL CRIME PREVENTION

2.5.1   It is often the case that situational crime prevention measures are not implemented or evaluated individually in relation to a single target or single problem. Instead, a crime or disorder problem might be tackled by using a package of measures. In such cases it is often difficult to define what precisely the crime prevention measure is or to determine what preventive impact various elements of the package have. In such cases it is probably more fruitful to conceive of the programme as a composite package rather than attempt to define and evaluate the component parts. The following example describes such an initiative in Canada.

THE HERON GATE PROJECT, CANADA

In Ottawa, Canada, five volunteer task forces were set up by the city's Crime Prevention Council to combat specific crime problems. One of these task forces was tasked with reducing crime in rented, high-rise housing blocks. The task force comprised tenants, apartment caretakers, representatives of the city police force and the executive director of the city crime prevention council. A range of situational measures were introduced including: target hardening, property marking and the creation of natural surveillance. In addition, tenants were encouraged to form apartment watch teams.

Caretakers or building superintendents helped to identify opportunities for reducing crime in their blocks which included checking the functioning of external doors and watching out for loiterers in the hallways or lobbies of buildings. The managers of the apartment blocks improved the security of doors and windows, removed signs of non-occupancy, improved the access control to the underground garage, and made environmental improvements outside the building such as improving outside lighting and trimming shrubs near the buildings.

Twelve months after the project had been implemented, the number of burglaries had fallen dramatically (Meredith, 1988). However, the number of vehicle-related incidents (damage to and thefts from) remained virtually unchanged, which was probably due to the fact that the measures to improve the security of the underground garage were only partly implemented.

2.5.2   One of the best examples of a multi-measure crime prevention programme which has recently been evaluated in terms of its impact on domestic burglary is the Safer Cities programme in England and Wales.

SAFER CITIES, ENGLAND AND WALES

Phase 1 of the Safer Cities programme (1988 - 1995) covered 20 cities in England and Wales. An evaluation of 16 of these cities with nearly 300 different prevention schemes targeting domestic burglary at the local level has recently been completed (Ekblom, forthcoming). Three-quarters of the local schemes focus on target hardening (including door, window and fencing improvements, entry systems and security lighting around individual houses or blocks). A further 8 per cent included other measures, such as raising the awareness of prevention amongst residents, providing crime prevention outreach workers, neighbourhood watch and property marking. A full-time-coordinator with a small team was employed in each city and a variety of local organisations were responsible for implementing the initiative at the local level. The evaluation focused not on individual schemes, but on the overall impact of preventive action in each local area.

Sources of information for assessing the impact of local action were recorded crime data and over 7,500 interviews with residents conducted on a before and after basis in 280 localities in 11 Safer Cities and 126 localities in 8 comparison cities. 96 of the local burglary prevention schemes were included in the survey- based analysis.

The survey results showed that, between 1990 and 1992, the risk of burglary fell in proportion to the level of action present in each locality surveyed. This fall was relative to background trends both in Safer Cities localities where no action had been taken and in comparison cities. Those areas in which the most action was taken experienced the largest declines in risk. Only minimal evidence of displacement has been identified, and the initiative appears to have been cost-effective in high-crime areas. However, little evidence was found that the schemes reduced worry about burglary.

Like the previous example from Canada, the evaluation was unable to distinguish which measures were most likely to account for the reduced risk of burglary. However, where additional funds were levered in from other sources (e.g. for housing improvements or other related activities), the effect on burglary levels was further enhanced. Likewise there were greater effects where target hardening was accompanied by other action.

2.5.3   The use of situational measures on their own can lead to a kind of "fortress" mentality, as residents become increasingly security conscious and withdraw into the perceived safety of their homes. This can be accompanied by increased feelings of isolation and fear of crime. Individual protection should therefore not be at the expense of measures to improve social interaction within the community. Initiatives like the Kirkholt project in England (see chapter 4), which latterly combined improvements in security and surveillance with community development and victim support work are more likely to improve overall levels of community safety. This broader, community-based approach to crime prevention is the subject of Chapter 3.

2.6   DISPLACEMENT

2.6.1   The issue of displacement is of central importance in evaluating situational crime prevention. There is strong evidence that situational crime prevention can prevent crime at its target locations. However, it is possible that all or many of the crimes prevented are simply committed at other times or at other places, leaving the overall crime rate unchanged. The original idea of a displacement phenomenon was first publicised in an article by Reppetto (1976) in which he hypothesized five forms of displacement: (i) temporal (committing the offence at a different time), (ii) tactical (committing the offence using a different method), (iii) target (committing the offence against a different target), (iv) territorial (committing the offence in a different area), and (v) functional (committing a different kind of offence). Since then, Barr and Pease (1990) have added a sixth category of 'perpetrator displacement', in which prevented crimes are committed by different offenders.

2.6.2   The proponents of situational crime prevention have made some attempt to identify weaknesses within the displacement argument, pointing out that displacement is neither inevitable nor necessarily unfavourable (Cornish and Clarke, 1988; Barr and Pease, 1990). The first argument draws on evidence from empirical research which typically shows that not all crime prevented is displaced. In a review of 33 studies, Eck (1993) found that 18 studies showed no evidence of displacement, while the remainder found evidence of either 'some' or 'much' displacement. No studies found evidence of 100 per cent displacement.

2.6.3   The second argument draws attention to the nature of the displaced offence. Barr and Pease (1990) argue that displacement can sometimes be benign as well as malign. Benign displacement may occur when the displaced offence is in some way less serious than the prevented offence. They provide as an example the possibility that gun control might lead to the greater use of knives in violent attacks. There is some evidence that the probability of a lethal outcome from an attack is related to the lethality of the weapon used, so displacement from guns to knives could be considered a socially desirable outcome. However, there are equally strong arguments for why displacement should continue to be taken seriously.

2.6.4   First, despite the clear and overwhelming body of literature which shows that situational crime prevention is effective in preventing crime at the level of individual targets, there is very little evidence to show that it can be effective at the level of whole estates, cities, regions or countries. It is perhaps surprising that for most of the period of development of situational crime prevention, international crime rates have increased. It is possible that the difference between the effectiveness of situational approaches at the target level and the city level is explained by displacement.

2.6.5   Second, despite the fact that many evaluations of situational crime prevention studies have investigated displacement effects, there are few studies which have attempted any kind of thorough search for displacement. A thorough search might include an attempt to investigate each of the six forms of displacement identified in the literature or it might include offender tracking to determine subsequent offence patterns of individual offenders following prevention (Eck, 1993).

2.6.6   Third, despite the fact that it is technically possible to conduct a comprehensive search of the kind described above, it remains methodologically very difficult to determine whether displacement has or has not occurred. The inability of research to detect displacement does not mean that it does not exist as its manifestation may be diffuse in terms of time, area, or type of crime (Gabor, 1990). While the concept of displacement most usefully refers to short term changes in crime patterns, it is possible that changes in opportunities for crime might result in longer-term changes in criminal behaviour.

2.6.7   The potential displacement effects of situational crime prevention cannot be ignored and the potential for displacement should ideally be built into the design of crime prevention programmes. Reppetto (1976) suggests that administrators of crime control programmes should be encouraged to specify the 'environmental crime impacts' of their programmes in order to predict the possible directions which displacement might take. In recent years there have been some proposals for tackling displacement as part of routine crime prevention activity, including the idea that likely displacement sites should be included in the crime prevention measure (Eck, 1993).

CHAPTER 3. COMMUNITY CRIME PREVENTION

3.1 INTRODUCTION

3.1.1   There is as yet no clear agreement on a precise definition of community crime prevention. For the purposes of this chapter, community crime prevention is defined as encapsulating both situational measures and measures to prevent criminality within a community-based framework of action. This working definition includes measures which emphasise the need to change the social, economic and demographic conditions which are believed to sustain crime in communities, including the development and strengthening of community institutions (Hope, 1994; Hope and Shaw, 1988), as well as measures which emphasise the need to involve members of communities in reducing opportunities for committing offences (Lurigio and Rosenbaum, 1986). It distinguishes between collective attempts organised at the community level and individual attempts organised at the level of individual households, victims or targets.

3.1.2   There are broadly three distinctive approaches to community-based crime prevention, although there is some overlap between them:

- Community organisation;

- Community defence;

- Community development;

3.2 COMMUNITY ORGANISATION

3.2.1   The 'community organisation' approach to preventing crime developed out of the work of the urban sociologists of the 'Chicago school' in the 1920s and 1930s, who developed the view that crime and delinquency are a product of rapid social change which causes a breakdown in informal social control. This approach was developed further by Shaw and McKay in the 1940s, who concluded that neighbourhoods with the highest delinquency rates were areas which experienced high immigration rates and which were in a constant state of transition. These changes resulted in weak social organisation and weak community identity, which in turn weakened the ability of the community to socialise and control its young people (Shaw and McKay, 1942). On the basis of this approach, a comprehensive programme to reduce crime through community organisation was implemented in the city of Chicago.

THE CHICAGO AREA PROJECT, USA

The Chicago Area Project (CAP), which was set up to prevent the development and continuation of criminality among young people, consisted of neighbourhood organisations, each with a self-governing citizen group operating under its own name and charter and governed by a local committee covering populations of between 10,000 and 50,000 residents. The principal aim of the local committees was to raise funds to conduct local neighbourhood activities directed at the area in general and young people in particular.

Each community committee was expected to conduct programmes designed: (1) to provide special facilities for work with groups of delinquent children at the neighbourhood level; (2) to bring local neighbourhood leaders into youth and community welfare programmes; (3) to aid the residents of the area in the development of a better understanding of the problems of children and youth through special adult education projects; (4) to assist local institutions and public officials to enlarge and make more effective services for the community; (5) to improve recreational, educational and other community services for children; and (6) to foster physical and social improvements of the neighbourhood.

In practice, the committees organised a wide range of programmes including: creating recreational and sports activities for children and young people, creating and using summer camps, securing access to churches and other local institutions, improving relationships between schools and the community through parent-teacher associations and adult education, running campaigns for community improvements, forming housing boards, involving the police and the courts in maintaining contact with delinquents, and incorporating young people on parole back into the community by giving them positions of responsibility within the community organisation (Sorrentino, 1959).

There is no real evidence to show whether CAP was effective or ineffective in reducing crime or delinquency, although both Kobrin (1959) and Sorrentino (1959) concluded that the achievements in community organising probably did reduce delinquency in the programme areas.

3.2.2   Two common problems in assessing the effectiveness of community crime prevention initiatives are firstly that it is difficult to disentangle observed changes from normal fluctuations in crime levels in small residential areas and secondly that it is often not possible to establish satisfactorily whether any reduction in delinquency is the result of the programme or other factors. Finestone (1976) noted that delinquency rates were lower in areas with strong community committees which, he suggests, was because strong communities were more easily set up in areas with low rather than high delinquency rates. He believed that the CAP evaluation illustrated that areas with high delinquency rates were much less willing and able to set up community organisations.

3.2.3   Despite the lack of empirical evidence to show whether community organisation was effective in reducing crime and criminality, attempts are still being made half a century later to reduce crime in residential areas by organising communities. In Chicago, renewed attempts at community organising which incorporate a much wider range of measures have been set up and evaluated. Ten community organisations were established and local residents were encouraged to collaborate in identifying and delivering activities ranging from block watch schemes and housing rehabilitation programmes, to recreational and job-counselling programmes for local youths and workshops on drug abuse. Four of these organisations were evaluated on a 'before and after' basis and all showed that social and physical disorder and fear of crime tended to be greater in the period *after* programme implementation than before. Hence, there was no evidence to show that community organising was effective in achieving any of its outcome goals.

3.2.4   A similar programme in Minneapolis, which employed professionals to train local leaders to organise crime prevention activities, produced similar results.

COMMUNITY ORGANISING IN MINNEAPOLIS, USA

Seven different areas of the city were identified as suitable for organising. Each of the seven areas was divided into three matched sub-areas. One of the sub-areas was randomly defined as the experimental area and was the target for the organising team's efforts. A second area was defined as an area for more intensive uniformed police work including police involvement in setting up block clubs. The third area was left to develop alone as a comparison area. Every household in the programme areas was visited during the course of the experiment.

The communities in the experimental areas were encouraged to conduct various kinds of crime prevention activities including: setting up block watch schemes, housing rehabilitation programmes, and recreational and job-counselling programmes for young people. It was found that people were generally willing to attend meetings and involvement in crime prevention activity increased in the programme neighbourhoods over the course of the experiment. There was also a substantial increase in awareness of increased community involvement. However, the results of the evaluation showed that there was no evidence of any programme impact on social disorder, crime, physical deterioration and fear of crime (Skogan, 1990).

3.2.5   The failure of these two contemporary programmes to show more positive outcomes is due, according to Skogan (1990), to the inherent difficulties of organising disadvantaged communities in high-crime areas. Programme participation and community activism were more common among people who lived in better-off, low-crime areas. Residents in disadvantaged areas find it more difficult to work in collaboration with the police and often do not have the resources to make community organisation work (Skogan, 1990).

3.2.6   These two contemporary programmes were based primarily (but not solely) on the principle that communities can be organised to reduce crime directly by engaging in crime prevention activities. However, the programmes discussed earlier in relation to the work of Shaw and McKay and the Chicago Area Project were based primarily on the principle that communities can be organised to reduce crime indirectly by strengthening the social processes which regulate behaviour such as informal social control. A programme in Puerto Rico, set up primarily to reduce criminality by providing services for high-risk youths, included community organising as a means of improving the general influence of the community on the socialisation and development of its young people.

EL CENTRO, PUERTO RICO

The programme at El Centro is an example of a community-based initiative which focused on both criminality prevention and community organisation. El Centro was based in the La Playa community in the city of Ponce in Puerto Rico. The centre was primarily a Youth Service Bureau with the nominal function of diverting young people from the juvenile court. However, under the strong leadership of the Centre's founder (Sister Isolina Ferre) the programme also took on a strong community organising role.

According to Silberman (1978), the philosophy of the programme was to change juvenile behaviour by changing adult behaviour. It was believed that the most effective way of changing adult behaviour was by creating a community organisation which enabled people to assume roles and responsibilities in relation to their own lives and their own community. At the start of the programme in 1970, the community was described as being disorganised to the extent that parents were unable to control their own lives or the behaviour of children in the area. Residents felt fatalistic and saw themselves as powerless victims.

The central component of the community organising part of the programme was the creation of a corps of ten full-time paid 'advocates' from among local residents. Their major role was initially to put pressure on public service bureaucracies to respond to the needs of the area. This later expanded to include more traditional community organising activities such as: organising recreational programmes, community outings, community meetings, and acting as mediator, in general community problem solving.

Silberman (1978) provides little evidence on the effectiveness of the programme in reducing crime or criminality. He reported that as a result of the juvenile diversion part of the programme that the number of adjudicated delinquents fell by 85 per cent during the early years of the project (the author does not state the precise period over which the reduction was made). He also reported that the delinquency rate had been cut in half (but provides no information on what this means or the period over which it applies). The most encouraging findings come from his descriptions of the qualitative changes in the life of residents in the area, who he believed had developed confidence and a sense of responsibility for their area. The descriptions are compelling, but without hard evidence it is difficult to know precisely what achievements have been made.

3.2.7   The effect of community organisation on informal social control has been assessed by Skogan (1990) and the effect of informal social control on crime and criminality by Greenberg et al., (1985). Skogan reports that participants in community organisations typically take more protective measures than non-participants and are more likely than non-participants to intervene in a crime event. However, there is less evidence to show that community organisation affects non-participants in the programme area. As community participation tends to be low (often less than 10 per cent) and participants tend to be less socially disadvantaged, he concludes that it is unlikely that community organising would have a widespread effect on informal social control.

3.2.8   On the effects of informal social control on crime and criminality, Greenberg et al. (1985) note that none of the evaluations on this topic actually measures informal social control. Instead, they examine measures of the social or physical characteristics of neighbourhoods which were believed to affect informal social control, such as: local ties, neighbourhood attachment, perceptions of control over the neighbourhood and the ability of residents to recognise strangers. The findings of these studies indicate that having friends in the neighbourhood, neighbouring activities, and the ability to recognise strangers are not related to crime rates. Emotional attachment to the neighbourhood, perceived responsibility for the neighbourhood, the expressed willingness of the resident to intervene in a criminal event, and the belief that neighbours would also intervene in a criminal event are associated with lower crime rates. However, it is unknown to what extent these characteristics are a cause or an effect of crime rates.

3.3   COMMUNITY DEFENCE

3.3.1   The 'community defence' model reflects a radical change in the nature of community crime prevention, which emerged during the early 1970s. Criminal policy moved away from the offender as the focus of intervention and towards the victim of crime. This change was accompanied by a shift away from the conception of a community as a structural and institutional entity and towards a psychological and symbolic entity (Currie, 1988). Whereas the strength of the former was measured in terms of the strength of its structures and institutions, the strength of the latter was measured in terms of people's attitudes towards it and in particular their fear of crime and how safe they felt on the streets (Currie, 1988).

3.3.2   The community defence approach was therefore influenced by a growing sense of fear of crime and personal insecurity within urban areas and the resultant increasing desire for self protection (Bottoms, 1993; Bottoms and Wiles, 1994). According to Wilson and Kelling (1982), people are fearful not only of crime but also of disorder. Disorder can take the form of disorderly people such as: beggars, drunks, drug addicts, rowdy teenagers, prostitutes, loiterers and the mentally disturbed; or of disorderly physical conditions such as: abandoned property, abandoned vehicles, broken windows, litter and weeds growing over public areas.

3.3.3   Disorder leads to fear of crime because it signifies a breakdown of community control. Residents begin to feel less safe within the community and begin to take defensive actions including retreating and securing themselves in their homes. It also triggers a developmental sequence in which petty crime, fights and public drinking lead on to more violent attacks, robbery and prostitution. At a certain point the area becomes vulnerable to invasion by criminals from outside of the area. Thus the community defence approach is characterised by a shift in emphasis away from 'the enemy within' (young delinquents living with families within the community) and towards an approach which focuses on 'the enemy without' (anonymous predators living outside the community) (Hope, 1994).

3.3.4   A programme in Newark, New Jersey, USA aimed specifically at tackling social and physical disorder by 'clean-up' campaigns and other measures is an example of the community defence model.

INTENSIVE DISORDER ENFORCEMENT, NEWARK, USA

Actions taken to reduce social disorder included: (i) 'Street sweeps' to reduce loitering and disruptive behaviour, drug sales and street harassment. The police were instructed to move on groups of four or more persons who might be defined as creating a public hazard. Loiterers were first warned using a loud-hailer from a police car and then by police search and arrest. (ii) 'Foot patrols' to disperse unruly groups of youths and enforce law and order on the streets. (iii) 'Radar checks' to enforce traffic regulations. (iv) 'Bus checks' to maintain order on buses and (v) 'road blocks' were used to deal with a number of motoring offences.

Actions taken to reduce physical disorder included the intensifying city services which involved increasing the speed of repair to buildings, making structural improvements, improving rubbish collection, and a 'clean-up' campaign. Additionally, juveniles convicted of petty offences were 'sentenced to the community' were allocated to some of these activities.

The results of 'before' and 'after' resident and area surveys showed that the programme had no impact on residents' satisfaction with the area or fear of crime and levels of reported physical disorder increased (Skogan, 1990).

3.3.5   The principal mechanisms for tackling social and physical disorder in Newark are based on police action (moving on and arresting groups of loiterers and increasing the number and frequency of foot patrols) and action by other agencies, such as the local transport department. Another dimension of the community defence model involves engaging local residents to patrol and surveille their own neighbourhood. Two principal components of the community defence model which have emerged are (i) citizen patrols and (ii) neighbourhood watch.

(I) CITIZEN PATROLS

3.3.5.1 In some countries, ordinary citizens form patrols to assist the police by watching from particular vantage points, checking on strangers and patrolling areas, often at night. They may check property and buildings and report deficiencies (e.g. open windows and unlocked car doors) back to the owners and suspicious incidents to the police. Citizen patrols vary according to location and area (individual buildings, estates, neighbourhoods, rural areas, transport systems, schools etc.), function (property protection, person protection, monitoring police behaviour and community safety issues such as fire prevention) and mode of transport (foot, vehicular).

3.3.5.2 In Russia, where the prevention and detection of crime is considered to be the responsibility of every member of society, citizen patrols (so-called 'public order squads') are commonplace. Large institutions and factories often have such a squad, the main purpose of which is to prevent violations of public order. Similar patrols exist in Hungary.

THE PECS PROJECT, HUNGARY

In Hungary, voluntary patrols have been introduced in combination with other crime prevention methods in a crime prevention experiment in a residential district of the city of Pecs. The principle aim of the project is to persuade residents to take better security precautions, although some offender-based measures are also being introduced (e.g. recreational activities for children at risk of offending). The patrols, which operate twice a month, consist of checking property and buildings in the district, reporting any deficiencies back to the owners (e.g. unlocked car doors) and informing the police if any incident occurs. No information is available on its effects on levels of crime or fear (personal communication from Ministry of Justice).

3.3.5.3 A variant of citizen patrols is parent patrols in areas where large numbers of adolescents gather, but again there is no evidence as to whether their presence prevents disturbances. Another variation is private patrols, which are paid for by local residents or the local council. Members (ordinary citizens) typically wear uniforms, carry mobile phones or two-way radios and receive special training. The activities of, and appointments to, such patrols need to be carefully regulated to ensure that they do not employ citizens with criminal records or engage in activities which are not within their legally defined powers.

3.3.5.4 In the USA, Canada and more recently in England 'Guardian Angels', comprising self-selected groups of volunteer citizens, offer their services to residential areas and transport systems and have received considerable publicity.

THE GUARDIAN ANGELS, USA, CANADA AND UK

They are different from ordinary citizen patrol groups in so far as they are specially trained, wear a uniform, physically intervene in criminal acts and make citizen arrests. Although unarmed, their appearance and functions closely resemble those of the police, which has evoked some criticism. Pennell et al. (1986; 1989) conducted a quasi-experimental evaluation of the activities of the Guardian Angels in San Diego using experimental and control areas. From the pre-test to the post-test period, the evaluation showed a reduction in violent crime of 22 per cent in the experimental area, but an even greater reduction of 42 per cent in the control area. A time-series analysis of monthly crime data did not indicate that the activities of the Guardian Angels and reported crimes were strongly correlated. Simple assault increased in the experimental area by two per cent compared with a nine per cent reduction in the control area. However, property crime decreased by a greater amount in the experimental area (25 per cent) than the control area (15 per cent). A community survey also showed that local residents believed that the Guardian Angels were effective and as a consequence felt safer knowing they were in the area.

3.3.5.5 One of the main problems with bodies like the Guardian Angels is that although they act within the law, they are not accountable for their actions in the way in which the police are. Their physical intervention in criminal acts has been the cause of some concern. The dividing line between acceptable and unacceptable public involvement is a thin one and citizen patrols may be accused of vigilantism, of unnecessarily intruding into areas of personal privacy, of usurping rather than assisting the police in their duty to uphold the law, of arousing suspicion amongst neighbours and of inadvertently undermining civil liberties. Constant vigilance and the introduction of operational guidelines should therefore accompany the expansion of surveillance in this form if human rights and freedoms are to remain unaffected.

3.3.5.6 Although citizen patrols may alert potential offenders to the fact that a community is continually being watched and reduce fear of crime, they have not yet convincingly demonstrated their effectiveness in reducing crime itself (Yin et al., 1977; Rosenbaum, 1988). The life expectancy of patrols tends to be limited; about half of the 226 patrols evaluated by Yin at al. (1977) ceased to operate within four years. Reductions in burglary have been recorded in residential areas in which citizen patrols have been operating (Titus,1984), but it is not known whether such reductions were caused by the patrols or by other factors.

(II)   NEIGHBOURHOOD WATCH

3.3.6.1 The essence of neighbourhood watch is to encourage citizens to become the "eyes and ears" of the police by watching out for and reporting suspicious incidents in their neighbourhood. The idea is that they should get to know each other, watch out for one another, intervene on behalf of one another in the event of witnessing something suspicious and report untoward behaviour to the police. Small groups of citizens come together to share information about local crime problems, exchange crime prevention tips and make plans for engaging in surveillance of their neighbourhood. Members keep an eye on each other's property, mark their goods, improve the security of their homes and in some programmes make suggestions for improving the physical environment. Other activities which can be included are victim/witness assistance schemes and block (or estate) parenting schemes, which provide safe havens for children in trouble. (See Garofalo and McLeod, (1988), for a full list of the diverse activities engaged in by neighbourhood watch programmes in the USA.)

3.3.6.2 A central principle of neighbourhood watch is that, by extending informal surveillance, reporting to the police and the number of arrests increases, the number of offenders on the street declines and other potential offenders are deterred from committing offences in what is perceived as a more risky area. By coming together to fight a common problem, the frequency and quality of social relations amongst residents improves, community bonds are enhanced and the community improves its capacity to defend the neighbourhood from predators. Furthermore, people's feelings of fear and powerlessness with respect to crime may be reduced and relations with the police may improve.

3.3.6.3 Neighbourhood watch programmes may be initiated by the police or a specialist crime prevention officer or, as is often the case, by members of the public. Police departments and particularly crime prevention officers are often key resources in neighbourhood watch programmes. They can provide residents with access to other public agencies, help them resolve local disputes and provide them with a source of authority and expertise. A local co-ordinator is usually appointed and individual estates within a neighbourhood may appoint representatives to act as intermediaries between residents and the local co-ordinator. Meetings and newsletters are used to keep members up to date and offer crime prevention advice, stickers are applied to the outside of dwellings to denote participation and street signs may be used to announce that an area is covered by a neighbourhood watch scheme. The US National Crime Prevention Council has produced a handbook on preventing crime in urban neighbourhoods, which provides a detailed, step-by-step account of how to set up neighbourhood watch programmes, what they should contain, how they should be run, who should be involved and how momentum can be sustained (N.C.P.C., 1986).

3.3.6.4 Originating in the USA in the 1970s neighbourhood watch has rapidly spread to Canada, the UK and, more recently, the Netherlands. Schemes may cover only a few residences or extend to thousands. Despite considerable interest in the concept of neighbourhood watch in principle, participation rates are quite modest, either because of lack of opportunity or lack of commitment. In the USA, 20 per cent of families live in an area where a neighbourhood watch programme exists and of these, just over a third actually participate in a programme (Garofalo and McLeod, 1988). According to Nuttall (1988), some 25 per cent of the population of Canada are covered by neighbourhood watch programmes and in the UK, 14 per cent of households report being members of a programme (Mayhew, Elliot and Dowds, 1989). In the Netherlands, neighbourhood watch programmes have only been introduced on an experimental basis (Lohman and van Dyke, 1988).

3.3.6.5 In general, neighbourhood watch is easiest to set up and sustain in homogenous, stable neighbourhoods where participation in voluntary and community organisations is common and residents tend to own their dwellings. Support for neighbourhood watch in such communities is more likely to come from people who are worried about becoming a victim of burglary, perceive the probability of victimisation as high, perceive their neighbours as friends or acquaintances and hold favourable attitudes towards the police (Hope, 1988; Bennett, 1989). Exchanging information about the nature and incidence of local crime and personal victimisation experiences can heighten fear of crime. In better-off neighbourhoods, care should be taken to ensure that neighbourhood watch does not exacerbate fear levels.

3.3.6.6 In more heterogeneous, unstable neighbourhoods with high proportions of residents from lower socio-economic groups, participation rates are considerably lower (see, for example, Shernock, 1986; Mayhew et al., 1989), although somewhat paradoxically, areas with low risks of burglary have higher rates of participation than areas with higher risks (Mayhew et al., 1989). In low participation areas, it may be necessary to broaden schemes to cover other issues or attach schemes to other pre-existing initiatives (Garofalo and McLeod, 1988). Husain (1988) discusses how schemes can be successfully established in areas of high crime and/or with low participation rates.

3.3.6.7 In practice, members of neighbourhood watch schemes do little more than put stickers or posters in their windows. Property marking and house security surveys tend to be taken up by only a minority of participants and levels of surveillance and rates of reporting to the police also tend to be infrequent (Husain, 1988; Bennett 1990). In an evaluation of neighbourhood watch in London, only about half of respondents who had looked out for something suspicious actually saw something and fewer than half of them reported what they saw to the police (Bennett, 1990).

3.3.6.8 An accurate assessment of the effectiveness of neighbourhood watch in reducing crime is complicated by the considerable number of poorly evaluated projects, many of which claim unequivocal success. Where sounder research designs have been used, the results tend to be less encouraging. In Seattle, the introduction of neighbourhood watch led to reductions in residential burglaries for participants during the first 12 months of the scheme. However, a telephone survey of the same residents 18 months after the implementation of the scheme showed that victimisation rates had returned to their original levels (Cirel et al., 1977). A project in Chicago produced even less encouraging findings.

THE CHICAGO NEIGHBOURHOOD WATCH PROJECT, USA

The Chicago project represents a comprehensive attempt to introduce neighbourhood watch in combination with opportunity reduction and informal social control elements coupled with a sophisticated evaluation design. The project was initiated by local volunteers from established community organisations in five neighbourhoods. A number of objectives were specified, including increasing awareness of and participation in the project, improving residents' sense of responsibility for and attachment to the neighbourhood, increasing social cohesion and reducing crime, incivilities and fear of crime.

The results of the evaluation, which comprised 'before and after' surveys of experimental and control areas, are not particularly encouraging. Although there was some variation between the five neighbourhoods, residents in those areas with neighbourhood watch tended to be no more likely to feel responsible for, or more attached to, their neighbourhood than residents in comparable areas where neighbourhood watch was not introduced. Areas covered by watch schemes differed little from those which were not in terms of levels of interaction on the street, watching one another's homes whilst away, home or self protection behaviours and intervention behaviours (Rosenbaum, 1988). More importantly, levels of crime and disorder remained largely unaffected by the programme and fear of crime tended to worsen in those areas where neighbourhood watch was implemented.

3.3.6.9 It has been suggested that since the evaluation designs were well constructed and the programme efficiently and effectively implemented, the apparent failure of the Chicago project may reflect theoretical weaknesses in the concept of neighbourhood watch (Rosenbaum, 1988). However, an evaluation of two neighbourhood watch schemes in England, which also found little evidence of reductions in crime, concluded that this was due to programme failure rather than conceptual flaws (Bennett, 1990).

NEIGHBOURHOOD WATCH, UK

In this initiative, the effectiveness of two neighbourhood watch schemes in two different areas of London were compared on a 'before and after' basis with two control areas, one of which was adjacent to one of the experimental areas in order to test for possible displacement effects. No positive effects were found on crime and little change occurred in either reporting levels or clear-up rates. Some improvement was recorded in levels of fear in one of the two areas and in both areas there were significant improvements in perceived satisfaction with the neighbourhood. One experimental area showed an increase in social cohesion, while the other experimental area showed an improvement in resident's involvement with others in home protection.

NEIGHBOURHOOD WATCH, UK (continued)

Bennett (1990) concludes that the effectiveness of public observation in small communities is probably very limited as many households are unoccupied for most of the day and many dwellings are poorly situated for maximising surveillance. Where there is a high turnover of residents, the identification of strangers becomes more difficult. The evaluation also established some doubt as to whether offenders were deterred by the knowledge that residents are supposedly looking out for suspicious activities. However, the area co-ordinator of one of the schemes thought that it had improved relationships between the police and the community and had brought the community closer together (which was confirmed by the survey analysis of the measures of social cohesion).

The overall conclusion was that programme failure was the most likely cause of the scheme's limited success. In practice, the majority of residents did little more than display window stickers and watch out for suspicious activities and little attempt was made to encourage regular, well attended meetings. There was no formal organisational structure, no newsletter, no meetings (formal or informal), few security surveys and only a limited property marking service. It was felt that there were too many other pressures on home beat police officers to design and administer the schemes properly.

3.3.6.10 Experience with neighbourhood watch appears to vary in different areas and according to how it is organised and implemented, but on the whole there is no conclusive evidence that potential offenders are deterred by the knowledge that an area is covered by a neighbourhood watch scheme (for the latest assessment of the effectiveness of neighbourhood watch, see Laycock and Tilley, forthcoming). Neighbourhood watch is perhaps more likely to be effective in preventing the development of a crime problem as opposed to dealing with an existing one.

3.4 COMMUNITY DEVELOPMENT

3.4.1   Community development has only recently been defined as a community based approach to the prevention of crime in its own right (Hope, 1994). Essentially, it comprises measures which seek to tackle urban disintegration by rebuilding the social, economic and physical fabric of communities which in turn may lead, intentionally or unintentionally, to reductions in crime and criminality. Four aspects of community-oriented programmes which might lead to reductions in crime and criminality through rebuilding communities are: (i) improving the built environment; (ii) decentralising housing estate management and services; (iii) improving housing allocation policies; and (iv) social and economic regeneration.

(I)   IMPROVING THE BUILT ENVIRONMENT

3.4.1.1   The possible effect of the built environment on crime has been discussed earlier in chapter 2. Accessibility, visibility and physical appearance have all been found to influence criminal activity (see, for example, Titus, 1984). Streets and dwellings which are easily accessible (i.e. near to car parks, main roads, street corners, recreation and commercial areas) or run-down, are more likely to experience crime and studies of vandalism in residential areas suggest that impersonal, easily accessible, semi-public/communal areas are more likely to be vandalised than other areas. However, the complexity, the expense and the contradictions inherent in carrying out environmental improvements limit their capacity to reduce or prevent crime. Measures for increasing visibility and reducing accessibility can, for example, also reduce privacy; similarly, measures designed to instill or increase a sense of territoriality, by for example erecting fences around public spaces, can reduce surveillability.

3.4.1.2   In this section, a broader range of changes to the built environment, which may affect whole communities as opposed to the residents of individual dwellings or blocks of dwellings, are considered. These changes are firstly to improve the design, maintenance and repair of buildings and their immediate surrounds and secondly to raise levels of building and investment in the area.

Design, maintenance and repair

3.4.1.3   The design and general level of maintenance and repair of an area influences the character of an area and the willingness of people to move into it and invest in it. There have been a number of attempts to improve the design and condition of the built environment at the community level as a means of bringing about crime reduction and other general improvements. The Hartford Neighbourhood Crime Prevention Program, for example, drew heavily on the ideas of Oscar Newman (1972) in restructuring a residential environment to bring about area-wide reductions in residential crime and fear. An evaluation of the impact of the programme as a whole showed a reduction in burglary and street robbery rates over the period of the programme (Fowler et al, 1979).

3.4.1.4   Osborn (1993), in a review of crime prevention programmes on housing estates in Britain, includes a number of projects which have included changes in design. He located eight examples of evaluations of design-led crime prevention initiatives. Four of these initiatives were said to have reduced crime, but only on the basis of anecdotal evidence. Two other projects which included the removal of walkways provided no strong evidence that the changes were associated with a reduction in crime. The remaining two showed some evidence of a reduction in crime although in the case of one this reduction was short-lived and in the other there was some doubt about the validity of the findings.

3.4.1.5 In Canada, the Royal Canadian Mounted Police (RCMP) have developed an approach to crime prevention in the province of British Columbia which is centred on the relationship between environmental design and crime. In addition to training courses on the relationship between architecture, town planning and crime, crime-prevention officers liaise closely with municipal planners, architects and administrators. However, without empirical evidence, it is difficult to know how effective the work of the RCMP in British Columbia is in reducing crime.

3.4.1.6 Ultimately, the mechanism through which changes in the physical environment impact upon crime levels is the effect such changes can have on the social behaviour of residents and consequently potential offenders. If, as a result of redesigning a neighbourhood, residents begin to become more involved in their community and with one another, then some of the conditions for reversing neighbourhood decline and improving the capacity of the community to defend itself may be developed. But without changes in other, predominantly social factors (e.g. number of young people, one-parent families, welfare dependants), crime is unlikely to be much affected. Oscar Newman himself modified his earlier work, acknowledging the importance of social factors (Newman and Franck, 1980).

Building and investment

3.4.1.7 Building and economic investment in a community is almost certainly an important factor affecting its general well being (including, physical appearance, social life and crime rates). The overall health of a community is governed by the level of confidence that people have in its economic base. An important factor in shaping this perception is the level of investment in the community, commercial interest in the area and the level of maintenance of the housing stock. An important motivator in this process is the level of corporate investment. Individual investment decisions made by home owners to maintain and improve their property will also be influenced by the investment decisions of the larger institutions within the community (Taub et al., 1984).

3.4.1.8 A striking example of the power of corporate investment to change the status of an area and reduce crime is shown in case of the Hyde Park area in Chicago, which included the main site of the University of Chicago. The change in community crime careers in the Hyde Park area was to a large extent the product of the actions of a single corporate body, the University of Chicago, which had an interest in improving the status of the area in which it was located.

HYDE PARK, CHICAGO, USA

At the beginning of the century, Hyde Park was a pleasant and thriving suburban residential community. The area developed further during the early part of the century to include the site of the world trade fair and the University of Chicago. By 1920, Hyde Park was fully developed and populated mainly by Irish, Germans, and Russian Jews. In the 1940s, blacks began to move into the area and by 1960 blacks constituted 30 per cent of the population. At about this time whites started to move out and the area gradually slipped into decline. Landlords failed to maintain their property and crime increased.

HYDE PARK, CHICAGO, USA (continued)

The response to the problem of deterioration was led by the University of Chicago, which owned property covering about 25 blocks of the Hyde Park area. In 1952, the University of Chicago set up the South East Chicago Commission and a process began of developing an urban-renewal programme. Ultimately, 30 million dollars were raised from federal funds along with 30 million dollars donated from the university's endowment. These funds in turn generated a further 90 million dollars of investment.

The investment was used to clear 47 acres of derelict housing from the areas, including run-down commercial strips and taverns. These were replaced with town houses and shopping centres. The university continued to be involved in the real estate market independent of the urban renewal programme and occasionally continued to purchase buildings threatened with deterioration and convert them into student or faculty housing. Similarly, the South East Chicago Commission continued to encourage private entrepreneurs to purchase buildings in the area and rehabilitate them (Taub et al. 1984).

(II) DECENTRALISING HOUSING ESTATE MANAGEMENT AND SERVICES

3.4.2.1 Research on the relationship between crime and housing is complex. The problems which generally characterise public housing are often quite different from those which characterise private rented or owner-occupied housing areas. The former tend to be high offender as well as offence rate areas and usually have quite different social compositions and histories. There are also variations within areas of public housing. Tenants in the poorest public housing estates are, according to Hope (1986), five times more likely to be burgled at least once a year than tenants living in better-off public housing areas. Other research has found that areas of similar design with similar tenure and resident income levels can experience very different crime rates (Bottoms and Xanthos, 1981; Bottoms et al. 1987). It is important, therefore, to ensure that the complexity of the relationship between crime and urban/housing policy is not simplified for the purposes of expediency.

3.4.2.2 Despite these difficulties, the trend towards consciously considering the crime preventive implications of urban planning policy has led to the development of a range of residential area improvement initiatives which combine environmental design criteria with housing management policies in both North America (McInnes et al. 1984) and Europe (Hope and Shaw, 1988; Vahlenkamp, 1989). The decentralisation of housing estate management and services amounts to a form of community empowerment and comprises the location of services on individual estate (including repair and maintenance) and consulting and involving tenants in the direct management of the area (Hope, 1994). The idea that decentralising housing management practice might lead to reductions in crime is based on the premise that such practices will not only help to improve the physical appearance and structure of the estate, but also restore a sense of control to residents and therefore increase their willingness and ability to develop community bonds and exert greater informal control over their environment.

3.4.2.3 A recent report (Osborn, 1992), which reviews the results of a large number of management-led housing estate programmes, concludes that management-led initiatives are successful in preventing crime when they are part of a broad programme of physical and social improvements, although none of the evaluations satisfied all the conditions of a satisfactory research design. The following is an early example of an estate management programme, which became a model for many subsequent developments in this area.

THE CUNNINGHAM ROAD IMPROVEMENT SCHEME, ENGLAND

The Cunningham Road Estate comprised 450 houses with a population of about 1,600 residents. Half the houses had been built in the 1950s and the other half in the 1970s. At the beginning of the project (towards the end of the 1970s) the older part of the estate was run down with some houses boarded up and others with broken windows. The shops were shuttered and daubed with graffiti and the estate generally was in poor condition (Hedges et al., no date).

The stated purpose of the scheme was to reduce vandalism and crime on the estates by involving local residents in improving the estate and the services provided. The project was based on the principle that any improvements made will be longer lasting and more effective if the wishes and priorities of the residents were taken into account and if they were made to feel responsible for the estate and the outcome of the project. Consequently, residents were invited to a number of public meetings during which their views on the estate were expressed and recommendations to the council were made. The improvements made included a variety of measures such as: traffic flow controls, modernisation and repair to the dwellings, improved policing, youth facilities, improved street lighting, litter removal and generally cleaning up the area.

The project was evaluated using 'before' and 'after' resident surveys and police and other official data. The research showed that the prevalence of burglary on the estate fell from 18 per cent in the pre-test year (1976) to 11 per cent in the post-test year (1979). There was also a reduction in the proportion of residents who said that they had noticed damage to dwellings (75 per cent to 53 per cent) or shops (67 per cent to 35 per cent) in the area. However, during the same period (1976 to 1978), police-recorded crime remained constant in the experimental area and reduced in the control area. It was concluded that there was some evidence of a reduction in crime, although the problem had clearly not disappeared.

3.4.2.4 More sophisticated initiatives employ co-ordinators to galvanise demoralised residents on run down estates to act together with local agencies and the police to improve both the physical and social conditions on the estate and reduce its vulnerability to vandalism, burglary and other crimes. Residents' associations are formed and encouraged to liaise closely with local authority agencies and play a central role in improving relations with the police. Housing estates which have been targeted in this way appear to have experienced reductions in crime and improvements in community safety, although not always without some displacement of crime to neighbouring estates or areas (Power, 1988). One such scheme, the Priority Estates Project, was set up to explore how best to resolve the problems associated with 'difficult-to-let' estates (see below), where tenant turnover is high, relationships between residents and the local council are poor and the estate is experiencing a 'downward spiral' of decline.

3.4.2.5 The two case studies presented above provide some evidence that community empowerment through estate management might be effective in preventing crime. However there is no explanation of how such programmes might have worked to prevent crime. As Rock (1988) has pointed out, it is difficult to understand in what way single or even multiple-measure interventions could alter the highly complex and variable social worlds of housing estates.

THE PRIORITY ESTATES PROJECT, ENGLAND

The experimental estate comprised a large housing development built in the 1960s which had become run down and in a poor state of repair with high crime rates. During the period of the evaluation (1987 to 1990) and following consultation with residents, various improvements were made as part of the programme. Estate and environmental improvements which were initially undertaken included: the addition of weather-resistance materials to dwellings, the addition of front gardens and fencing, blocking-off walkways, adding CCTV to the entry system in high-rise blocks of flats and environmental landscaping. Subsequently, the main elements of the PEP model of decentralisation of services and tenant management were introduced, including: the formation of a local steering committee, estate-based management, caretaking, cleaning teams and repair teams. Finally, the estate experienced an increase in new tenants over the study period which affected the social mix of the area.

The evaluation was based on pre-test and post-test resident surveys and site observations and interviews. The research found that the prevalence and incidence of burglary on the estate reduced over the period of the study, while burglary rates on the control area increased. The reduction in burglary (and vandalism) was most noticeable in the area of the improved houses on the estate. The prevalence of burglary among the unimproved houses reduced by a smaller amount, whereas the prevalence of burglary in the tower blocks on the estate increased.

The authors concluded that different parts of the programme had different effects on different parts of the estate. It is possible that the reduction of burglary in the unimproved houses was a result of resident involvement and empowerment serving to increase social control. The reduction in burglary in the improved houses on the estate was perhaps a product of opportunity reduction through informal surveillance and control. The increase in burglary in the tower blocks was perhaps due to a change in social mix in the area which served to intensify criminality among the existing criminal population (Hope and Foster, 1992).

(III)   IMPROVING HOUSING ALLOCATION POLICY

3.4.3.1   In this review, housing allocation policy is discussed separately from the community improvements and community empowerment approaches discussed above. In practice community strategies draw on a number of approaches and often combine each of the above types of programme. However, housing allocation policy is conceptually distinct from the other two and is often included as a separate component of more general community crime prevention strategies.

3.4.3.2   The rise of mass public housing schemes in Europe since the end of the Second World War has brought with it concern at the high rates of offending and victimisation which seem to characterise such schemes. Bottoms and Wiles (1988) suggest that one of the reasons for these high crime and victimisation rates is that housing allocation mechanisms concentrate together certain groups of people - often the poor and most disadvantaged - in the same areas. They describe a process known as 'tipping', whereby popular, low crime estates can rapidly 'tip' into unpopular, high crime estates which then become 'difficult-to-let'. Once an estate acquires such a reputation, the process becomes self-fulfilling and only the most desperate and least discriminating families will be willing to live there. Bottoms and Wiles (1988) suggest that policies of dispersal or tenant mixing and the early identification of 'tipping' may help to prevent the development of 'difficult-to-let' estates.

3.4.3.3   There are few examples of attempts to improve local areas and reduce crime and criminality specifically though changes in housing allocation policies and procedures. There are, however, some projects which include housing allocation policy changes with other community development strategies. Burbidge (1984) notes that several local authorities in England have taken measures to reduce concentrations of children or disadvantaged households on particular estates and Osborn and Bright (1989) point to the importance ensuring that families with children are allocated to low-rise blocks. A programme implemented in the Netherlands includes careful consideration of the social mix of the area in its general improvement strategy for a public housing estate.

THE BREDA PUBLIC HOUSING INITIATIVE, THE NETHERLANDS

In the Netherlands, a scheme to redevelop a high-rise public housing estate in the city of Breda through physical and environmental improvements found that crime and fear of crime did not improve. On the contrary, it continued to worsen and as a result of persistent pressure from tenants, the authorities implemented a series of changes to housing management and housing allocation procedures and introduced a range of social measures to improve living standards and create a stronger sense of social cohesion within the neighbourhood (Kalle, 1987). Caretaking and maintenance functions were decentralised to estate offices and the local authorities made sure that new tenants were "suited" to the neighbourhood. A social plan was drawn up by the tenants and the authorities working together, which included measures for tackling vandalism and crime and improving community safety.

THE BREDA PUBLIC HOUSING INITIATIVE, THE NETHER-LANDS (continued)

Each block appointed contact persons with the tasks of introducing new tenants, explaining house rules, etc. and neighbourhood assistance committees were set up to facilitate complaints procedures and act as a forum for tenants to discuss potential improvements. These changes were further complemented by the introduction of procedures to ensure that the responsibility for putting right any damage caused to the buildings or the surrounding environment is passed on to the offender, whether a tenant of one of the blocks or not. More frequent police patrols were also instigated and the police agreed to react quicker to complaints. Finally, an information campaign was set up to keep tenants informed of developments, such as the way those who had committed damage made reparation and what the dangers and consequences of drug use and dealing are.

(IV)   SOCIAL AND ECONOMIC REGENERATION

3.4.4.1   The above example from the Netherlands serves to illustrate the importance of not only monitoring neighbourhood crime and victimisation rates, but also of differentiating between different kinds of neighbourhood in various stages of decline. There are clearly some neighbourhoods which are so entrenched in a cycle of decline, that only a combination of physical, environmental, managerial, social and economic measures are going to be effective in reversing the process. Mobilising support and co-operation in such communities is often difficult. A high proportion of local crime prevention schemes suffer from a falling off in enthusiasm and participation and experience has shown that community-based crime prevention initiatives often drift into tackling other, more important problems, especially in the most disadvantaged areas. Skogan (1988) suggests that it is often more productive to attach crime prevention initiatives to other community issues around which the community has already organised, but where such organisations are totally lacking or poorly supported, no less than a comprehensive programme of social and economic regeneration may be required.

3.4.4.2   Early attempts to alleviate poverty and lack of employment opportunities in urban slum areas through large scale community development in the USA (Mobilisation for Youth, and 'War on Poverty') were unsuccessful. In the UK, similar attempts to meet the needs of people living in areas of high social deprivation by changing the social and economic conditions which structured their lives were found to be politically, administratively and financially over-ambitious. Hope and Shaw (1988) succinctly sum up the reasons for the failure of grand scale social engineering programmes:

> *"The political conflict involved in these projects, their consumption of resources, their perceived lack of tangible effect, their grandiose designs and aims, and their raising of expectations within the community which could not be met, all fuelled a reaction against 'social engineering' for crime prevention purposes."*

3.4.4.3 During the last decade, national attempts at social and economic regeneration in North America and Europe, during a period in which the welfare state and the principles of welfarism have been in general decline, have generally given way to locally based, low-key and sometimes piecemeal initiatives, which are deliberately generated at the grass roots level rather than imposed upon local communities from above. The focus of these initiatives has, by and large, been on the need to integrate young people at risk of offending back into the community. The key institutions which need to be mobilised include networks of families, peers and neighbours and local institutions such as schools and places of employment and, if they exist, voluntary and other community organisations. Some of the more successful strategies which such institutions can employ were discussed in C hapter 1.

3.4.4.4 To a large extent, the success of community-based crime prevention programmes based upon local policies which attempt to alter the social and economic fabric of neighbourhoods, will ultimately depend on the development of, or at least support for, the same policies at both national and regional levels. However, there is some room for local communities to manoeuvre within the overall constraints of national and regional social and economic policies. Resources for combatting crime can be specifically targeted on those areas which need them most; residents in high crime areas can learn how to use existing resources more effectively; administrative arrangements can be re-organised in order to focus resources more closely on the needs and problems identified by local inhabitants; the devolution of political power can help local citizens achieve their objectives more readily and effectively. Thus there is scope for developing local strategies for combatting crime which go beyond altering the physical environment and influence the social, economic and cultural conditions associated with crime in particular areas.

3.4.4.5 Bright (1992) describes a programme conducted in the Bronx area of New York City by a particularly active community group. The target area of the group had experienced over 25 years of disinvestment, housing abandonment and population loss. The area had spiralled so much into decline that 'arson-for-profit' by landlords had become a daily occurrence. The group worked with local government officials in creating a community revitalisation programme for the area. The programme included restoration of services, renovation of abandoned buildings and development of housing projects. In addition the programme involved working with local business people in an attempt to improve the physical appearance of the local commercial strip and to foster growth of new business. According to Bright (1992) the area experienced a growth in population and the vacancy rate of commercial buildings fell from 50 per cent to zero.

3.4.4.6 The conditions for reducing or preventing crime tend to be least favourable in communities which suffer the most from crime and fear of crime. Given this dilemma, decisions concerning the targeting of crime prevention resources - whether, for example, to concentrate on those areas which need the resources most or those areas where efforts are most likely to succeed - must be taken with care. The question of how to optimise the targeting of crime prevention resources is the subject of considerable debate (see, for example, Wilson and Kelling, 1982; Currie, 1988). One difficulty which arises is how to make accurate assessments of the precise state of the physical and social health of neighbourhoods in order to make correct investment decisions; not all declining neighbourhoods require the same level of investment to turn decline around. Cost-effective policy making demands solutions which match the scale, and the nature of problems. Thus crime analysis (see chapter 4) needs to be combined with a community audit, which establishes the needs, problems and local resources of the community, before policies are designed to tackle crime and criminality.

3.4.4.7   However, it is recognised that the capacity of such communities to organise a collective response to crime and to socialise residents, especially immigrants and the young, into a community consensus of norms and values, is severely limited (Garofalo and McLeod, 1988). Where high crime areas are characterised by strained or antagonistic relations with the police, mobilising community support and generating a greater sense of "community", which depends on building a basis of trust and co-operation between residents and the police, may be very difficult. In areas like this, where the consent of those being policed is absent, policing may even be counter-productive. The role of the police in community crime prevention is discussed in the following section.

3.5   THE ROLE OF THE POLICE

3.5.1   Actions taken by the police to prevent crime or disorder in community areas which are based on consultation or collaboration with members of the community constitute an important element in community crime prevention. The work of targeted police patrols was discussed in the previous chapter on situational crime prevention as they tend to operate at the level of specific targets or locations rather than as attempts to prevent crime at the level of whole communities. There are two approaches to policing which can form part of a community-based strategy to the prevention of crime: (i) community policing and (ii) problem-oriented policing.

(I)   COMMUNITY POLICING

3.5.1.1 The concept of community policing represents a significant shift away from traditional law enforcement models of policing. The essence of community policing is to improve the accessibility and visibility of the police by providing a more permanent and grounded presence in the community and to develop closer and more responsive relationships with citizens. The three main elements of this relationship are 'consultation', 'collaboration' and 'consent'. The idea of the police consulting with the public means that the police listen to the community in order to improve the quality of the service they offer and to assist in determining priorities and operational policy. Collaborating with the community refers to a relationship in which the police and the public work together, in partnership, to achieve common goals. Obtaining the consent of those they police requires the police, within a formal system of public accountability, to explain and be accountable for their actions.

3.5.1.2 Research on the effects of community policing has been somewhat equivocal, both with respect to its effects on crime and police/public relations. The degree to which community policing has been implemented is itself questionable and in practice there have been very few evaluations of community policing which have addressed the issue of crime prevention. The preventive impact of community policing can be effective at two levels - at the police department or area level and at the operational or local level.

Area level strategies

3.5.1.3 The main area level strategy is decentralisation and includes programmes such as sector policing and team policing. Research on the crime prevention effectiveness of decentralisation and team policing has produced mixed results. A study by Wycoff and Skogan (1993) of community policing in Madison showed that burglary rates reduced while robbery rates remained unchanged following the introduction of the programme. A study by Capowich and Roehl (1994) of community policing in San Diego showed no reduction in crime following the implementation of the programme, whilst an evaluation of the Cincinnati Team Policing experiment (Schwartz et al., 1977) showed a reduction in certain categories of crime during the programme, including reductions in burglary. A study in Britain actually showed an increase in the number of victimisations and multiple victimisations during the course of the experiment (Irving et al., 1989). Thus it has yet to be proved that community policing can prevent crime at the area level.

Local level strategies

3.5.1.4 The two main community policing strategies at the local level are community constables and police shops. Community constables are dedicated police officers who are allocated to a particular area (usually a single beat) on a permanent or semi-permanent basis with the specific task of providing a full police service to the local community of that area. A recent national survey of community policing in Britain, which examined (amongst other things) the work of community constables, found that they were widely used, but that the scheme suffered from varying degrees of implementation failure (Bennett and Lupton, 1992b). Community constables were frequently withdrawn from their beats to conduct other and unrelated duties in other areas and less than 10 per cent of their time outside the police station was spent on community contact or preventive work (Bennett and Lupton, 1992a). There have been no evaluations of the effect of community constables on crime rates (although there are a number of evaluations of the impact of foot patrols on crime, which were referred to in chapter 2).

3.5.1.5 Police shops (or mini stations), which are usually located in vacant premises in residential areas (usually in the vicinity of other community organisations) or town centres, are intended to increase accessibility to the police and awareness of policing issues. Police shops in town centre areas (but not in town centre shopping areas) typically act as a base for advertising crime prevention advice or for promoting the latest police crime prevention campaign.

3.5.1.6 Police shops (referred to as storefronts in the USA) were part of the broader programme of policing evaluations in Newark and Houston in the USA (Pate et al., 1986, but see also Skogan and Wycoff, 1986). The Houston initiative, which was evaluated using pre-test and post-test victimisation and public attitudes surveys, found that respondents were generally aware of the existence of the station and experienced a proportionally greater reduction in fear of crime and perceived area crime problems than residents in the control area. However, there was no significant reduction in victimisation levels. In Canada, police shops are used widely as part of their recent move towards community policing. The following comprises a summary of one such initiative, the COPS programme (Community Police Stations), in Victoria.

THE VICTORIA COMMUNITY POLICE STOREFRONTS, CANADA

The stated aims of the programme were to reduce crime and fear of crime by increasing community accessibility to police services through the development of police storefronts (Walker et al., 1992) One constable was permanently assigned to each storefront station along with 15 to 20 volunteers to staff the station. The volunteer staff manned the station two at a time on four-hour shifts. The constable reported to the programme manager. All stations implemented various programmes such as: neighbourhood watch, Block Watch and DARE (Drug Abuse Resistance Education) for children aged 10 to 12 years.

An evaluation of the programme showed that it was highly regarded as being worthwhile for parents and the police. However, there was no evidence to suggest that attitudes of the children to the police or to the community became more positive as a result of the programme. Overall, the authors of the evaluation concluded that the programme failed to meet in any significant way the general philosophy and goals of community policing, as well as the needs of the community being served.

3.5.1.7 Overall, research has identified at least four ways of improving community policing (see also Goldstein, 1987).

- The nature and focus of crime prevention work within the police profession needs to be clarified and enhanced, particularly amongst the lower ranks. The idea that the main function of the police is to detect mainly serious crime, irrespective of its frequency in, or impact on, local communities, needs to be qualified. To enhance the status of community policing in general and beat policing in particular, the advantages of proactive work and the disadvantages of reactive work need to be clarified.

- To produce a sensible balance between reactive and proactive policing, it may be necessary to enhance proactive work. The introduction of other performance indicators in addition to arrest and process reports could assist in this. These could include the development of productive contacts with local groups and agencies and changes in reporting levels and clear up rates for those crimes of most concern to the public.

- Police training should focus more on increasing professional skills relevant to community policing, especially the development of communicating and organising skills, on work with other agencies and on community relations work, especially with minority groups and work with the young and the elderly.

- In so far as police effectiveness depends upon public co-operation, the police should construct strategies to prevent those crimes and public nuisances which are of greatest concern to the community. The police should not and cannot "own" the crime problem, so strategies should be developed together with residents and local agencies. The police should keep the public informed about developments. Local surveys can be used to establish what the community's priorities are, what the community expects and demands of the police and which areas are most at risk of crime and victimisation.

(I)   PROBLEM-ORIENTED POLICING

3.5.2.1 Problem-oriented policing involves the routine application of a systematic approach to problem solving across a whole department involving all officers. It requires a more specific definition of problems than that offered by legal offence categories, with descriptions which include information gathered from a wide range of sources on, for example, the location and time of specific incidents and the behaviour and motivation of the people involved (Goldstein, 1987). Problem-oriented policing orients the planning and implementation of policing to community problems, including incidents which may fall short of breaches of the law. The heart of problem-oriented policing lies in what Eck and Spelman (1987) call the problem-solving process, which has four stages: (i) scanning, (ii) analysis, (iii) response, and (iv) assessment. (Further detail concerning the principles of problem-oriented policing are outlined in Goldstein (1990) and Eck and Spelman (1987).) As with community policing, it is possible to consider whether problem-oriented policing is effective in preventing crime at the area and the local or target level.

Area level strategies

3.5.2.2 There is little evidence available on whether problem-oriented policing is effective in reducing crime at the area level. The only evidence available is from Britain (Bennett and Kemp, 1994), in which an evaluation observed 18 months or so of the early stages in the development of sector-based, problem-oriented policing in two areas. The effect of the programmes on crime in each of the two areas was evaluated using pre-test and post-test victimisation surveys and showed that neither the prevalence nor the incidence of victimisation reduced over the period of the evaluation.

Local level strategies

3.5.2.3 There are slightly more evaluations of individual attempts at problem solving. Eck and Spelman (1987) examined three schemes in Newport News, USA. All three programmes resulted in crime reductions. The following comprises a summary of one scheme.

NEW BRIARFIELD APARTMENT COMPLEX, NEWPORT NEWS, USA

The New Briarfield Apartment Complex of over 400 single-story, timber-framed dwellings was arranged in groups of four to 16 apartments. The dwellings were built during the Second World War as temporary accommodation for shipyard workers. The housing was not intended to be permanent, but remained after the war as a result of general housing shortages. In 1981, the complex had the highest burglary rate of any residential complex in Newport News. The police decided to take some action to reduce the burglary rate.

One of the officers involved in the case contacted a number of local agencies and held a meeting to discuss the future of the complex. The heads of the agencies agreed that it was not practicable to renovate New Briarfield as the buildings had deteriorated too much. Burglary was a problem in the area largely because the doors and windows did not fit their frames properly, leaving a space around them for burglars to lever open. A multi-agency group set up by the police engaged in various negotiations with the owners of the property with the view to renovate and maintain the properties. The apartment owners and the city agencies collaborated to clean up the area. The owners agreed to renovate and improve the properties as far as was realistic in the short term. The residents also set up a neighbourhood watch scheme and worked closely with the police in monitoring crime in the area. A long-term plan was agreed with the local authorities and the property owners eventually agreed to rebuild the properties and move the residents out. An analysis of crime in the area showed that the early interventions had resulted in a reduction of burglary in the complex (Eck and Spelman, 1987).

3.5.2.4 A study by Hope (1994) examined the effectiveness of three examples of attempts by the Metropolitan Police Department of St Louis, USA to implement problem-oriented policing in order to solve drug and related problems in residential areas. All three showed evidence of a decline in calls for service following the intervention. The following again comprises a summary of one of the projects.

PROBLEM-ORIENTED POLICING IN ST. LOUIS, USA

The first case study involved a drugs problem in a deteriorated 'sub area' of an otherwise stable and racially integrated neighbourhood in St Louis. The problem investigated related to a single address within a block known to be the location of a street drug market. The problem location resulted in over 100 calls for service within a six month period. The police arranged various actions to tackle the problem including collecting additional information by video recording the area at night and compiling maps of dwellings. The team tackling the problem convened a meeting of property owners in the area and discussed various actions to be taken. The most substantial action taken was a successful effort on the part of the police to persuade the owner of the problem address to sell the property. At the point of handover of ownership, the police helped evict the existing tenants. A plot of calls for service over the programme period showed a reduction in calls associated with the problem address, while calls relating to other addresses in the block increased. The author concluded that the programme was effective at the site of the problem address, but appeared to result in displacement of problems to surrounding addresses (Hope, 1994).

3.5.2.5. Overall, the research findings on problem-oriented policing are fairly positive. In addition to improvements in the amount and relevance of information generated by such an approach, it would appear that it can reduce crime at the local level. However, it can suffer from implementation difficulties (Hoare et al. 1984) and there may be problems of displacement to neighbouring areas (Rosenbaum, 1988). Nevertheless, the problem-oriented approach is being increasingly incorporated into the crime preventive process, which allows resources to be tailored to specific patterns of offending in their local contexts (Ekblom, 1988). The crime preventive process is the subject of the next and final chapter.

CHAPTER 4. PLANNING, IMPLEMENTING AND EVALUATING CRIME PREVENTION

4.1   INTRODUCTION

4.1.1   The previous three chapters have discussed the nature and effectiveness of crime and criminality prevention strategies once a programme has been devised and implemented. However, the process of devising and implementing crime prevention programmes is important in determining programme effectiveness. Rosenbaum et al. (1985) argue that programmes might fail to be effective for a combination of reasons including 'theory failure' (when the programme is not capable of initiating the required mechanisms even when fully implemented) and 'programme failure' (the programme does not constitute the right kind or right 'dosage' of intervention to initiate the required mechanisms). Hence, implementing crime prevention programmes requires selecting strategies which are both appropriate and sufficiently robust to bring about the desired changes in crime.

4.1.2   This chapter provides a guide to the process of crime prevention including the design, implementation and evaluation of crime prevention measures. It focuses on the kind of crime prevention that can be done at the local or small area level (e.g. individual residential communities) rather than at the level of whole cities, regions, or countries. The main reason for this focus is that crime is not randomly distributed across geographic areas but tends to be concentrated in specific crime areas, locations or 'hot spots' (Sherman et al., 1989). Studies of drinking and disorder in Britain, for example, have found that offences are most likely to occur near drinking establishments, particularly just after they close and on Friday and Saturday evenings (Hope, 1985; Tuck, 1989). Crime events can also be clustered within high crime areas and within specific locations of high crime areas. Ekblom (1986) found in a study of shoplifting that three-quarters of all offences observed by store detectives occurred in three out of 40 sections of the shop.

4.1.3   In recent years, a number of practical guides on how to choose and implement crime prevention strategies at the local level have emerged (Eck and Spelman, 1987; Ekblom, 1988; Shapland et al., 1994). These guides all recommend that local groups responsible for crime prevention should first identify the nature of the problem before designing potential solutions. All three are similar and differ only in emphasis and how they organise the process.

4.1.4   Ekblom (1988) uses a five-stage sequence of activities. The first stage involves *collecting data* from a number of sources in order to provide information about the problem to be tackled. The second stage involves *crime analysis* which aims to identify patterns of crime from the data gathered. The third stage is concerned with *identifying appropriate prevention strategies* from what is known about the processes involved in the creation of the problem. The fourth stage involves *implementing* the strategies and the fifth stage involves *evaluating* the extent to which the strategies were effective and, where appropriate, feeding back to adjust strategies in the light of experience.

4.1.5   A more recent guide to the crime prevention process written with practitioners and local multi-agency groups in mind has been produced by Shapland et al. (1994) on targeted strategies for local areas. Their approach adds a useful additional dimension to Ekblom's approach by detailing targeted approaches for implementation in small areas, which compliment city-wide and national initiatives. The following sections, which are based on Ekblom's approach but also draw on the approach by Shapland and her colleagues, describe how to design, implement and evaluate crime prevention strategies.

4.2 INFORMATION GATHERING

4.2.1   The information gathering stage should not be limited to the crimes or incidents which it is intended to prevent. The information should cover:

- information about the area within which incidents occur or target offences are committed;

- information about the actors involved (victims, offenders, third parties) and the incident/target offence itself (physical setting, social context, sequence of events and results of the events);

- information about responses from others (the community, businesses, institutions);

- information from interviews with offenders to enhance knowledge about the logistics of crime.

4.2.2   The collection of information on the area within which incidents or target offences occur might involve compiling maps of the area derived from physical surveys. Such maps or surveys should reveal information about the following (a selection of some of the proposed items to investigate):

- the extent, type and location of residential property,

- routes through the area used by pedestrians and vehicles, including unofficial paths,

- some idea of traffic flow and where people park their vehicles,

- some idea of the social use of the area,

- possible problems in the area, including litter and the state of repair of buildings.

4.2.3   Further work on who is involved and what is happening where, will include the collection of information on:

- Offender characteristics (i.e. age, sex, class, race, whether alone or accompanied, criminal record, criminal contacts, school and employment record, family status etc.)

- Target or victim of the offence, such as car, bicycle, domestic goods and age, sex and lifestyle of victim, including activity at time of offence (e.g. commuting, shopping, sightseeing).

- Nature and location of offences, including legal categorisation and contextual information, such as motives and grounds for dispute, physical proximity (e.g. near railway station, in shopping precinct) and location (e.g. on platform, in subway).

- Timing and method of offending, such as date, day of week, time of day, point and means of gaining entry.

- Physical and social circumstances of the offence (i.e. lighting, degree of crowding, presence of potential interveners etc.) and whether the offence was successful or not.

- Cost (financial and social) of the offence and associated damage and type of goods stolen or damaged.

- Involvement of alcohol and drugs as motive and contributory victim behaviour, such as negligence or provocation (Ekblom, 1988).

4.2.4   The importance of collecting comprehensive and detailed information on the nature and patterns of crime before going on to devise preventive strategies is illustrated by the following burglary prevention initiative in Rochdale, England.

THE KIRKHOLT PROJECT, ENGLAND

This project to reduce burglary on a very high risk local authority housing estate combined target hardening measures with target removal, victim support, security surveys, property marking and measures to improve informal surveillance. The project based its approach on data gathered from in-depth crime, offender and victim surveys. It was administered by a number of agencies working together, including the local authority housing department, the gas and electricity utilities, the local victim support organisation, the Manpower Services Commission and the local crime prevention group with representatives from the estate itself.

THE KIRKHOLT PROJECT, ENGLAND
(continued)

The information from the surveys proved invaluable for the subsequent design of appropriate preventive measures. Convicted burglars were interviewed about a range of factors including distance of the burglary from home, the reasons for choice of target, time and circumstance of the offence and the reasons and motives for the burglary. Burglary victims and their immediate neighbours were also interviewed and provided information on, for example, visibility of the burglar's point of entry, levels of security hardware and their use, occupancy and its signs at the time of the burglary and previous victimisations.

By contrasting the location and other characteristics of victimised households with obvious alternative targets (i.e. neighbouring victimised dwellings of similar physical appearance), preventive measures could be specifically targeted on dwellings and parts of dwellings of greatest vulnerability. Thus it was found, for example, that victim houses were more likely to be burgled again than neighbouring houses, which led to a deliberate focus on multi-victimised dwellings. Similarly, it was discovered that more than two-thirds of entry points were visible from the neighbour's dwelling, which led to the setting up of mini neighbourhood watch schemes (mini or 'cocoon' neighbourhood watch schemes differ from the standard neighbourhood watch scheme in so far as they are triggered by a specific event and form around small, close groupings of dwellings).

Other insights which informed the design of preventive measures included the fact that burglars tended to travel very short distances to commit crimes and tended to specialise in certain types of houses; and that signs of occupancy, highly visible entry points and visible burglar alarms all acted as deterrents.

The initial results of the evaluation showed that over the first year burglaries declined by more than 50 per cent and multiple victimisations reduced almost to zero. Only recorded offences of vandalism increased on the estate following implementation of the project. It has been suggested that this may have been due to an increase in pride in the estate and confidence in the police, leading to a greater willingness to report incidents of vandalism.

4.2.5   Data about crime are routinely collected by a number of agencies and organisations, including local government and some national organisations, but the main source of information about crime is the police. Their information comprises data based on offences, offenders and their records of routine and emergency calls and is potentially of great use in guiding small groups in devising crime prevention strategies. Recorded police data usually contains information about the legal category of the offence, where it occurred (sometimes this is geo-coded to facilitate crime mapping), the time and date of the offence, whether an offender was detected and details of the offence including whether property was stolen and its value. Where relevant, further information may also be included on the type of dwelling, the entry point (in relation to burglary), the type of goods stolen or damaged, the presence or otherwise of witnesses and the age and sex of victims. However, because police data is not primarily compiled for guiding the development of preventive strategies, the data may fall short in terms of completeness, continuity, reliability and validity.

4.2.6   There are two main problems with using police offence data. Firstly, not all offences are reported to the police and secondly not all offences reported to the police are recorded by them. Inevitably, this leads to underestimations of the amount of crime committed in a particular area. In addition, they may also serve to distort the distribution of crime if some groups (perhaps those who are less satisfied with policing in their area) report a smaller proportion of offences to the police than other groups. However, for practical purposes, these problems will not seriously hamper detailed crime analysis of an area.

4.2.7   Information about where offenders reside is particularly useful for estimating offender rates for particular areas and determining connections between area of residence and area of offending. Research suggests that offenders tend not to travel far from their place of residence (perhaps no more than one or two miles at most) and tend to offend in familiar places which are close to the routes and areas covered during their 'routine activities' (Brantingham and Brantingham, 1993).

4.2.8   Information about routine and emergency calls from the public to the police can provide additional information about incidents, especially those which do not result in any formal action being taken (e.g. some violent offences, especially domestic disputes). The disadvantages of using such data are that the nature of the incident is often not clearly specified (including its legal status) and if the information is computerised, a substantial amount of the information may be 'lost' (i.e. large numbers of incidents tend to be recorded in residual or 'miscellaneous' categories).

4.2.9   One important area on which data should be collected is repeat victimisation. In recent years, new information about repeat victimisation has been uncovered which has very important implications for crime prevention. Research shows that a relatively small proportion of the population experience a relatively large proportion of all victimisations. Farrell and Pease (1993), for example, found that about 20 per cent of the population of England and Wales experienced about 80 per cent of all victimisations and a number of studies have found that victims of crimes such as burglary, racial attacks and domestic violence, are at a much higher risk of being re-victimised than non victims, especially in the immediate aftermath of the original victimisation (Polvi et al., 1990, 1991; Sampson and Phillips, 1992; Farrell, 1992). Furthermore, research has also shown that the proportion of repeat victims in high crime rate areas is substantially greater than the proportion of repeat victims in low crime areas (Trickett et al., 1992).

4.2.10   Police-recorded crime may also not be an accurate source of information about repeat victimisation. For example, repeat victimisations tend to be even more under-reported than other offences and, where an address turns up repeatedly in police incident logs, the chances of recording errors increases (for further problems, see Farrell and Pease, 1993). These and other imperfections, which are not uncommon to other forms of data, should be taken into account in designing research strategies based on police-generated data on repeat victimisation.

4.2.11   Police data can be supplemented by offender surveys, observation and information on 'good practice' elsewhere. Information on the public's definition of the crime problem, their priorities for action, their views of the police and the provision of services by other local agencies can be collected through surveys and observation and can be used to gain valuable insights into offender behaviour patterns. Surveys can also be used to assess whether specific areas or groups of people have been successfully targeted by preventive measures. Special training in the basic techniques of data collection and analysis and a reasonably high organisational priority to information gathering needs to be achieved for the preventive process to be an effective and routine part of crime management.

4.3   ANALYSIS AND INTERPRETATION

4.3.1   The crime analysis stage of the preventive process consists of two components. The first involves summarising the data on offending and victimisation and trying to discover patterns among them, whilst the second involves interpreting patterns of offending and victimisation and attempting to explain them (Ekblom, 1988). The analysis may be based on one particular offence (e.g. robbery) or on more than one type of offence.

4.3.2   One of the most effective ways of identifying crime patterns is by creating crime maps of an area which overlay crime data and area characteristics, such as the sites of schools, pubs, main roads and other factors which might be relevant in explaining the pattern. Maps can be constructed by a number of methods, from placing pins on a street map to using sophisticated computer mapping programs. The main advantage of the latter is that it allows large numbers of maps to be created relatively easily once the programme and data have been set up, although computer mapping requires some investment of time (and hence cost) in entering the data and setting up the programme. Such crime maps can be used to identify crime 'hot spots'. Research has shown that crime is not evenly or randomly distributed in terms of time and space, but tends to be clustered (Sherman et al., 1989) and identifying and explaining crime clusters can help to determine appropriate preventive strategies. In Sweden, maps have been used in Stockholm to locate, amongst other things, delinquent peer group networks and the places where they congregate (Sarnecki, 1992).

4.3.3   Another method of analysing and determining patterns in crime is to construct graphs of crime over time. Establishing that a large proportion of assaults occur between the hours of 10-00 p.m. and 2-00 a.m. on Friday and Saturday nights might, for example, provide useful guidance on how to prevent it. Such graphs can be in the form of simple daily, weekly, monthly, or yearly time plots and can be designed to identify rapid changes in the rate of commission of crime at certain points in time. These points might be correlated with other changes such as the release of one or more prolific burglars from custody or with a depletion in police manpower on the streets due to some large public event drawing on their resources.

4.3.4   The final stage of the analysis concerns interpreting the patterns observed. To achieve this, information and patterns observed in relation to crime need to be combined with information and patterns observed in relation to physical, social and demographic data. Some minimal knowledge of criminology and theoretical crime and criminality prevention might be helpful here. It is possible, for example, that a crime 'hot spot' might be the result of particular opportunities generated by the location or it might be the focus of routine activities of potential offenders in the area.

4.4   DEVISING STRATEGIES

4.4.1   Once the pattern of crime has been established and interpreted it is necessary to think about methods for intervening in order to disrupt the pattern or interrupt the causal chain which would otherwise have led to the criminal event (Ekblom, 1994). Agencies will need to choose at what point in the causal chain an intervention should be placed. Thus interventions could be 'distal' in the form of actions taken to influence the early development of young people at risk of becoming offenders, or 'proximal' in the form of actions taken to influence the immediate situation of the offence (Ekblom, 1994). Distal strategies might include those discussed in the earlier chapters on criminality prevention and community crime prevention, whereas proximal strategies might include those discussed in the chapter on situational crime prevention.

4.4.2   At the 'social' level of intervention (which might include programmes aimed at both criminality and community prevention), a decision should be made as to which institution should be the agent or target of the preventive action (e.g. the school, the family, the job market). At the 'situational' level of intervention, a decision should be made about which element of the situation should be the target of the action (e.g. the potential target, capable guardians,or the environment of the offence).

4.4.3   Where patterns of repeat victimisation have been identified and analysed, measures targeting known victims and/or their dwellings or premises may need to be devised. Targeting known victims leads to a higher 'hit rate' of those likely to be victimised in the future and protects the most vulnerable social groups without having to identify them first. One example of a programme which has explicitly targeted repeat victims is the Kirkholt Burglary Prevention Project, which provided security surveys and hardware and encouraged victims to join cocoon neighbourhood watch schemes (see chapter 3). Other measures to prevent repeat victimisation include offering victims of burglary or assault portable intruder alarms or a video system capable of identifying burglars (Farrell and Pease, 1993).

4.4.4   Crime prevention groups should also have a clear idea about which 'causal mechanisms' might operate to ensure an intervention's success. The installation of CCTV cameras in public places might reduce crime in a number of different ways, including encouraging more people to use the streets, increasing the rate of apprehension of offenders and deterring potential offenders. Local crime prevention groups should also be aware of which causal process it aims to influence in order to assess the effectiveness of the programme.

4.4.5   Once the level of intervention and the nature of the causal mechanisms have been identified, the choice of measure to implement could be selected from a list of packages suitable for that kind of intervention. Such a list has been usefully provided by Ekblom (1994). In many cases, the most appropriate intervention may require no more than fairly mundane actions, such as repairing buildings, enforcing local regulations and building codes and activating individuals or agencies to take responsibility for their property (Hope, 1994).

4.4.6   Determining priorities for intervention may pose problems. Issues to consider will include the relative practical benefit to the community of different measures and the social and economic costs of the criminal activity under consideration. Resolving the question of priorities will need to be undertaken in accordance with local circumstances, although where the analysis of crime and the allocation of preventive resources covers a large urban area or indeed a whole town, this may require the setting up of a special committee or commission.

THE ENQUETE COMMISSION, GERMANY

In 1979, a special independent Commission was set up to carry out a systematic analysis of crime and its causes in the city of Neumuenster and to present practical recommendations for the development of preventive measures. Referred to as the Enquete Commission, it worked closely with (although independent of) the town's authorities to develop a picture of its social and urban structure and crime problem. The commission used local police statistics, self-report data from a sample of local schools, a survey of offender characteristics and an analysis of the spatial distribution of offences as data bases. Their report provides a comprehensive list of social and situational measures for preventing and reducing crime, including the setting up of a city-based inter-departmental committee for crime prevention and a pilot project for examining the effects of introducing 'community stations' in specific high crime neighbourhoods on a ratio of one for every 250 residents. Their responsibilities would include increasing local involvement and participation, improving community relations, encouraging self help initiatives, resolving local conflicts, providing crisis intervention and legal, financial and personal advice on a 24-hour basis.

A crucial pre-condition for setting up 'community stations' was found to be the procurement of financial and political support from the local Mayor and his/her chief administrator. In Neumuenster, it proved difficult to convince local politicians and administrators of the financial benefits of preventing rather than reacting to crime after the event. This occurred partly because there was no evidence on the success or otherwise of 'community stations' in reducing crime. In practice the implementation of the Neumuenster project was also severely hampered by conflicting tensions between different agencies, and especially between the police and social workers with respect to the problem of juvenile crime. Simplified, the police tended to perceive young delinquents as 'being' a problem, whereas social workers tended to perceive them as 'having' a problem (Graham, 1988c).

4.4.7   As the above example shows, sometimes inter-agency tensions and individual agency interests can influence not only which measures are selected but whether a programme even gets off the ground. The selection of measures should nevertheless be based on rational assessments of their likely effectiveness rather than their administrative or political convenience. Research and evaluation can assist agencies to select appropriate measures and methods of working which transcend such difficulties. If possible, crime (and community) analysis should also attempt to anticipate some of the constraints which may arise in the implementation of crime prevention initiatives.

4.5   IMPLEMENTATION

4.5.1   Five main strategies can be used for implementing crime prevention measures; (i) the use of regulations to enforce norms of conduct, such as the passing of bye laws to restrict the purchase and consumption of alcohol at certain times or in certain places; (ii) the provision of facilities and practical assistance to support desired actions, such as the installation of computers for monitoring non-attendance levels at schools; (iii) the use of incentives to encourage people to adopt measures, such as lower home insurance premiums for those who install door and window locks; (iv) negotiation to resolve differences of interest, particularly between agencies operating at the local level and the people for whom they provide a service; and (v) through advertising and disseminating information and advice. Which strategies are adopted will depend upon the nature of the problem and the particular difficulties which need to be overcome to achieve effective implementation. In practice, however, effective implementation is often difficult to achieve and incomplete or insufficient implementation is unlikely to be effective in reducing crime.

4.5.2   The problem of implementation is less pronounced where only one agency is involved. So, for example, the police have been fairly successful in implementing high-profile patrols, saturation patrols and under-cover teams in attempts to detect or deter offending (Eck and Spelman, 1987; Hope, 1994). But the problem of implementation is more pronounced when a number of agencies come together to devise and implement a crime prevention strategy. A demonstration project, which aimed to test the feasibility of a range of measures to reduce vandalism in eleven primary and secondary schools, documented some of the problems involved in multi-agency attempts to implement crime prevention (Hope, 1985).

SCHOOL VANDALISM DEMONSTRATION PROJECT, ENGLAND

Groups comprising school staff, local authority officials and the police, were given responsibility for deciding which measures to adopt at each school in order to tackle school vandalism. While the groups were given advice by the Home Office on a range of both situational and social measures which could be taken, they invariably chose physical situational measures. Hope notes that the reason for this choice was not because these measures were necessarily thought to be more effective by the groups. Instead, Hope argued, they were chosen largely because they were administratively more convenient to implement and fitted more closely the preconceived beliefs of group members concerning the nature of the problem and appropriate preventive solutions.

SCHOOL VANDALISM DEMONSTRATION PROJECT, ENGLAND (continued)

In practice, few of the measures chosen were fully implemented. Only half of the 30 measures ultimately chosen had been implemented after two years and only two schools implemented all measures. In three schools none of the proposed measures was put into practice.

Five main obstacles to implementation were identified:

(1) Unanticipated technical difficulties

Most of the schools recommended installing damage-resistant glazing as a replacement for existing glazing. However, not one pane was installed in any of the schools as the City Architects prohibited this type of glass from being fitted on the grounds that it would impede exit during a fire.

2) Absence of control over local activity

One school decided to redesign the school grounds to divert congregations of children to less vulnerable areas. This decision involved the approval of the education department and the city planning department in the council. After 18 months neither had reached a decision.

3) Failure to co-ordinate action

It was recommended that residents living near to two of the schools should be encouraged to keep an eye on the schools after school hours and to report anything suspicious to the police. The decision to achieve this depended on the support of the education department, the headteacher, the staff and children at the school, and three branches of the local police. The groups approved the idea of the scheme but no group was willing to take the lead and to coordinate the activities.

(4) Competing priorities

The difficulties of implementing the schemes were not only the result of what the authors call bureaucratic inertia. The agencies involved in the scheme were all undergoing internal reorganisation of one kind or another. The anti-vandalism projects were dropped in terms of their priority among all agencies involved in favour of the existing organisational priorities of the agency.

(5) Inhibiting consequences

This refers to the wider consequences of any actions taken. These included such things as the effect of paying caretakers in one school overtime payments to patrol the school. This resulted in other caretakers in the region demanding overtime payments. Ultimately the costs of the scheme and the trouble caused by demands for overtime in other schools resulted in the scheme being scrapped.

4.5.3   Other studies have documented some of the difficulties encountered when agencies come together to implement crime prevention strategies. A crime prevention programme in South West England, which used a joint action group comprising the church, the council, local agencies and the police to prevent crime and develop community initiatives, experienced various inter-agency difficulties (Moore and Brown, 1981). These included conflicting professional approaches to the problem, a lack of knowledge about each others' roles, perceived threats to an agency's sense of independence and authority and encroachment on areas of responsibility and territory.

4.5.4   Power differentials between participating agencies are inevitable, but need to be tempered wherever possible. It is particularly important that the "police view" does not become the dominant view to the exclusion or partial exclusion of the views of other interested parties. Relations between multi-agency committees and local residents also require careful handling as they may also have conflicting priorities. It is particularly important to ensure that the views of minorities are not submerged under the views of more powerful groups since these minorities may well be the prime victims of crime.

4.5.5   Despite the wide range of problems associated with implementing crime prevention measures, there are ways in which these problems can be addressed. Firstly, the structure of the crime prevention organisation should be sufficient to enable the various functions of the organisation to be performed. These structures need to be flexible enough to consider crime and criminality prevention at various levels from county to individual street. Effective groups are often drawn together by a leading individual or group. The police often take the leading role in crime prevention initiatives, but this need not always be the case. While the police or some other department of the local authority may tend to take the lead at the city, county or district level, a wide range of organisations or even individuals can take the lead at the project level. The securing of resources is also an important element of a successful crime prevention programme (Home Office, 1990).

4.5.6   Secondly, multi-agency networks can be quite complex, so they need to be effectively directed and managed by a professional co-ordinator who should monitor progress, stay abreast of developments and act as a catalyst, a negotiator and a motivator. Co-ordinators can be appointed from one of the agencies in question or externally. Both have advantages and disadvantages. External recruited coordinators may mean extra expense and they may antagonise agency workers who resent perceived interference. Co-ordinators appointed from one of the agencies, on the other hand, may upset the balance of power between agencies, particularly if a consensus on goals and ways of achieving them have not yet been settled.

4.5.7   Thirdly, it is important to ensure from the outset that the local community accepts joint responsibility for initiating and sustaining crime prevention programmes. To assist in this, a community-based participatory forum can be set up to underline and facilitate the sharing of responsibility, increase public awareness, facilitate joint decision-making and support the initiation and co-ordination of action. Caution should be exercised to ensure that agreements reached during the decision-making stages are not progressively watered down or undone during implementation. Open forums can assist in this by bringing potential conflicts out into the open before implementation begins.

4.5.8   Fourthly, where the focus of activity is on the prevention of criminality, a long-term perspective will need to be adopted, which may conflict with the demands of local inhabitants for an immediate response. The success of such initiatives requires a continuing commitment and effective leadership, whether by a lead agency or a group of committed volunteers. The durability of the group can also be assisted by developing a clear structure and strategy for the future.

4.5.9   Programmes which adopt largely situational measures are easier to implement and sustain. They are less dependent on a consensus of values, are more likely to be seen as a direct response to crime and offer solid incentives for maintaining participation. However, as described above, they can also be hampered by implementation difficulties and may even have the opposite effects of those intended. One of the most important potential side effects of situational crime prevention initiatives is that the careless, badly designed deployment of physical and surveillance measures can inadvertently lead to a "fortress" mentality, which increases fear of crime and can worsen a community's criminal reputation.

4.5.10   Finally, implementation can be made more effective if programmes are routinely monitored. By continuously assessing what is happening and making adjustments accordingly, monitoring allows those who manage programmes to stay abreast of developments rather than lag behind them. As far as possible, routine monitoring should be organised in such a way that the collection and collation of information is tailored to the requirements of evaluators (see below).

4.6   EVALUATION

4.6.1   The final stage in the crime prevention process is evaluation of the project or programme which has been implemented in terms of its impact on crime levels. Evaluations need to be carefully planned before the programme begins, allowing enough time for implementation to occur and outcomes to be measured. Interventions to prevent criminality may need considerable time to work through. If the period is too short, not enough time may have elapsed for the the effects to be felt. A decision has to be taken on who is going to conduct the evaluation. Should it be conducted by those involved in the programme itself or should the evaluation be conducted independently? Self-evaluations are cheaper but suffer from a temptation to distort the findings towards a successful outcome. Evaluation loses its value and its credibility if it simply becomes a catalogue of good news, so mistakes and indeed failures need to be recorded with integrity. Independent evaluations tend to be more expensive, but they give the evaluation a degree of credibility which will often be worth the extra expense. Some assessment will also need to be made of the likely cost - about 10 per cent of the programme's total budget has been suggested (Doig and Littlewood, 1992) - and in some cases it will be necessary to convince fund holders that money spent on evaluation is money well spent.

4.6.2   A distinction between two parts of the evaluation process is commonly made. The first part is usually referred to as a process evaluation and comprises an assessment of the way in which the programme was implemented in practice. The second part is usually referred to as an outcome or impact evaluation and its aim is to determine to what extent the programme impacted on the event it was designed to influence. The former process requires monitoring the implementation of the programme and in particular what happened (as opposed to what was meant to happen). The latter process involves measuring the impact of the programme on the outcome variables (e.g. levels of crime) targeted by the initiative.

(I)   PROCESS EVALUATION

4.6.2.1 A process evaluation needs to identify what happened over the course of the intervention and in so doing highlight the difficulties encountered. The method of evaluating implementation effectiveness will vary by type of programme. In an evaluation of truancy patrols, the number of young people stopped on the streets by the police was used as a measure of programme implementation (Ekblom, 1979), whilst in an evaluation of neighbourhood watch, a cluster of indicators were measured, including: whether a window sticker was displayed, whether residents defined themselves as members of the scheme, whether they had marked their property, whether they had home security survey, and whether they had looked out for anything suspicious and reported it to the police (Bennett, 1990). An experiment which aimed to determine the effect of police presence at the site of local crime 'hot spots' employed research student observers to stand in the epicentre of the 'hot spot' and count the presence or absence of police cars during each minute of an observation period (Koper et al., 1992). The following description of the process evaluation of a major crime prevention initiative in the USA provides an interesting example of how important lessons can be learnt from such evaluations, even where programmes are hardly implemented.

THE ANTI-CRIME PROGRAMME, USA

In 1985, the U.S. Department of Housing and Urban Development's Anti-Crime Programme identified a wide range of factors as causing or facilitating crime, including poverty, relative deprivation, limited employment opportunities, institutional racism, poor education, inadequate housing, broken homes and reduced family functioning. Working in partnership with the Departments of Labour, Justice, Interior, Health and Human Services and Local Government, the programme was built around the premise that urban deterioration and crime go hand in hand and that crime-free and orderly neighbourhoods can only be secured through the social control activities of citizens supported by official agencies. To achieve this goal, a wide range of crime prevention measures were identified including housing management, tenant organisation, employment initiatives, programmes for youth, women, the elderly and victims of crime and better policing. These formed the basis of anti-crime initiatives in 16 cities, which were often similar in design, but varied considerably according to local determinants.

THE ANTI-CRIME PROGRAMME, USA (continued)

The main objective of the process evaluation was to determine what happened in each project. How much activity was generated? What was its character? What factors determined the form, content and timing of various programmes? Kelling et al., (1986) have provided a detailed account of the findings of the process evaluation, the most important of which may be summarised as follows:

(i)   There is no clear, linear progression from policy-making to implementation. The former was found to be an on-going process which overlapped with and sometimes grew out of the latter.

(ii)   Implementation varied substantially between the 16 cities. In some, activities were delayed, modified or re-defined altogether; in others, some activities were ignored in preference to others or only token efforts were undertaken.

(iii)   The assumption that crime and fear of crime was both serious and prevailed equally in all 16 projects was unfounded. This false assumption led to each project receiving the same funding without having regard to demand or scale. Consequently, the seriousness or otherwise of the problem overwhelmed a project in one area, but made it irrelevant in another. This underlines the importance of starting with a systematic analysis of crime and how it is perceived by local residents in each area, before making decisions on strategies, measures, funding and the targeting of resources.

(iv)   The confusion as to whether the initiative was being financed on a temporary or more permanent basis led to different agencies viewing and using the programme in different ways. The former felt that limiting the programme to 12-18 months meant it could not be properly implemented and their level of commitment and subsequent activities were influenced accordingly. Lack of skills in planning and co-ordinating the initiative also led to conflicts between participating agencies.

(v)   The role of the police was found to be central to the success of the initiative. Police commitment was viewed by many residents as an indication that the authorities were taking the problem of crime seriously and their involvement led to greater demands for a police presence, especially foot patrols and team policing.

(vi)   Employment initiatives came out as by far the most successful elements of the programme, since creating training and employment opportunities was perceived as important in its own right, not just because it might reduce crime.

4.6.2.2 Criminality prevention programmes are often implemented within a multi-agency framework and this can lead to a number of difficulties. Different agencies have different professional approaches and may be relatively ignorant of the roles and responsibilities of other agencies. Some agencies may feel their independence and authority threatened by participation in a multi-agency forum, whilst others may be oversensitive to what they perceive as an unnecessary encroachment on their territory. Multi-agency networks can unwittingly lead to duplication, bureaucratic inertia and unhealthy competition for scarce resources. All these and no doubt other conflicts of interest may produce what is known as 'project drift' in which the programme's original objectives are gradually redefined or dropped altogether. If intermediate objectives have been set, then it may be that the evaluation is still able to report a partial success.

4.6.2.3 There are ways in which some of these problems can be minimised or overcome. The most important of these are to make sure that an appropriate lead agency is identified from the beginning, to involve the community and/or the target group in designing and implementing the programme, to ensure that the programme is monitored and that the information this generates is effectively fed back into the implementation process and to employ professional coordinators rather than leave coordination to chance.

(II) OUTCOME EVALUATION

4.6.2.4 Outcome or impact evaluation tends to be based on a more limited range of methods. The most common evaluation designs to determine the impact of social interventions on outcome measures are (i) experiments and (ii) quasi experiments.

Experimental Designs

4.6.2.5 The key difference between experimental and quasi-experimental designs is that in the case of the former the researcher has control over the assignment of the programme or intervention under test to experimental or control conditions, while in the case of the latter the researcher does not have this control. The classic experimental design thus comprises allocation of subjects to experimental and control groups. Pre-test measurements are taken before the experimental intervention is implemented in the experimental group. Post-test measurements are then made after the programme has had time to take effect. Differences between the experimental and control groups may then be attributed to the programme, since this comprised the only known difference between the two groups.

4.6.2.6 In the case of experimental designs, the programme or intervention may be assigned to the experimental or control conditions by random allocation, by matching or by some other method of purposeful selection. Experimental designs involving randomised assignment are the most valid methods of determining causality between the 'treatment' variable (e.g. the crime prevention strategy) and the outcome variable (e.g. the crime rate). This is because all other variables which might affect the outcome variable (e.g. the effect of sex, age and socio-economic status on the probability of victimisation) can (in principle) be controlled by the randomising procedure.

4.6.2.7 Relatively few randomised experiments can be found among evaluations of crime prevention programmes. One of the most well known studies of the effect of a policing strategy on crime using randomising techniques is the Kansas City Preventive Patrol Experiment, in which fifteen beats were randomly divided into three experimental conditions: five reactive beats (officers respond only to calls for service), five control beats (one car per beat), and five proactive beats (with two or three cars per beat) (Kelling et al., 1974). Measurements were taken during the period before the programme was implemented and again after it had been running for just over one year.

4.6.2.8 The Kansas City evaluation found no impact of the programme on crime or victimisation and has been widely criticised on the grounds that it did not fulfil all of the conditions of an experimental design. Fienberg et al. (1974) doubt whether the beats were randomly allocated in the conventional sense (equal probability of subjects or areas being selected) as the reactive beats were at the corners and in the middle of the experimental area. Pate et al, (1975) believed that the police selected the configuration of beats to best suit their operational interests. Farrington (1983) doubted whether random allocation of just 15 items across three experimental conditions would be sufficient to ensure equivalence between the experimental and control conditions.

4.6.2.9 In practice, true experimental designs involving random allocation are difficult to establish. For example, it is not always possible to control allocation of the key independent variable (the intervention, treatment or programme); there are normally many other criteria for guiding allocation of interventions to areas or groups and in some cases it may be unethical to allocate resources to one group of people or one area and not another. As a result, evaluators of crime prevention programmes tend to use something less rigorous than the full experimental design.

Quasi-Experimental Designs

4.6.2.10 When it is not possible for the researcher to control the allocation of a programme or treatment to experimental and control conditions, it still may be possible to investigate the effects of the intervention as if it were an experiment. This may occur when, for example, residents in an area decide to set up a neighbourhood watch scheme or when the government decides to change the law relating to drinking while driving. The researcher cannot control who receives the programme, but may nevertheless investigate the effect of the intervention by looking at experimental and control groups, or by looking at pre-intervention and post-intervention measurements. Under these conditions, the researcher may conduct a 'quasi-experiment' to determine the effect of the programme.

4.6.2.11 Quasi-experimental designs, although probably the most common design in evaluation research, are somewhat inferior to true experimental designs because they cannot control for the effects of any extraneous factors which may influence the dependent variable (e.g. crime rate). This means that it is difficult to know whether any difference between the experimental and control groups shown in the post-test period is the result of the intervention or not. In the terminology of research methodology, quasi-experimental designs suffer more than experimental designs from threats to internal validity. It is necessary, therefore, to engage in a formal process of interpretation in which the evaluator must consider the mechanisms that might link the variables under test and the likelihood that the presumed cause generated the measured effect. In practice, this might mean determining whether the introduction of a crime prevention programme caused a reduction in crime or whether something else happened in the area that affected crime rates. It might also mean ascertaining whether the programme could have instigated the mechanisms that might have led to a reduction in crime.

4.6.2.12 In contrast to experimental designs, the threat that people (or other units) in the experimental and control group might be different in some way is also a problem in quasi-experimental designs. For example, the research evidence suggests that people who join neighbourhood watch schemes are not the same as people who do not. The former are more likely to be home owners, to live in houses rather than flats, to be married and to have children under the age of five than non participants (Bennett, 1989). Fortunately, some (but not all) of the problem of non-equivalence can be controlled during the analysis stage of the evaluation. In general, evaluators using quasi-experimental designs should therefore be aware of the main threats to validity when interpreting findings (see, for example, Pawson and Tilley, 1992 and 1994) and attempt to deal with them as far as possible as part of the research process (see Cook and Campbell, 1979; Judd and Kenny, 1981).

4.6.2.13 Despite these drawbacks, quasi-experimental designs have many advantages which make them attractive as a method for evaluating crime prevention programmes. For example, it is possible to evaluate the effect of a crime prevention strategy even when the researcher has no control over where the strategy is to be implemented. There are therefore many quasi-experimental research designs which can be adopted by the researcher when an experimental design is not an option. Four of the most common designs are described below.

4.6.2.14 The one-group pre-test: post-test design involves observations before an intervention, during implementation and after the intervention (see, for example, the Kirkholt Burglary Prevention Project (Forrester et al., 1988). However, the design does not allow the evaluator to establish what might have happened in the absence of the intervention. It cannot be assumed that crime rates will remain constant in an area from one point in time to another, so it cannot be stated whether a reduction in crime is more or less than would have been expected anyway. The main design problem is that since extraneous factors are not controlled, it cannot be said with any degree of certainty that the change in the outcome variable (e.g. crime rate) is the result of the intervention or the natural history of the area or group, which might have led to such changes anyway.

4.6.2.15 The problem of the effect of 'history' and extraneous variables on the outcome variable can be overcome to some extent by including a control group. The untreated control group design with pre-test and post-test measurements is perhaps the best compromise between methodological adequacy and practical necessity (see, for example, the evaluation of neighbourhood watch in

London by Bennett, 1990). The distinguishing features of this design are that similar pre-test and post-test measurements are made in an area or among a group without the intervention and the units measured (e.g. residents interviewed) are different in the pre-test and post-test surveys (this is most likely to occur when separate cross-sectional surveys are conducted).

4.6.2.16 This design is stronger than the single group design as it helps control for the effect of 'history', which may affect both the experimental and control area. Thus if crime rates were falling anyway, this would be shown by a reduction in both the experimental and control areas. The unique effect of the intervention on the crime rate could then be observed as the difference between the reductions in the experimental and control areas. However, the design does not control for what is sometimes referred to as 'local history', which affects only one of the areas. Insufficient attention to local historical events during the course of the Kirkholt Burglary Prevention Project evaluation, for example, resulted in the authors failing to notice that a substantial area improvement programme was also operating during the experimental period (Osborn, 1992). As a result, it is now unclear whether the reductions in crime reported in the programme area were a result of the burglary prevention programme or these other events. In order to reduce the effect of 'local history', it is necessary to monitor the experimental and control areas and to take any changes observed into account when interpreting the results.

4.6.2.17 The above design can be varied slightly to improve the equivalence of the pre-test and post-test samples by measuring the same units (e.g. interview the same individuals) on both occasions. However, attempts to re-interview the same respondents across two time periods often results in a heavy attrition of cases, which undermines the representativeness of the sample. As a result, this method (sometimes referred to as a panel sample design) is best used to determine changes among individuals, whereas the previous design (sometimes referred to as a cross-sectional sample design) is best used to determine changes within areas. In practice, both methods can be used in order to achieve the benefits of each.

4.6.2.18 The interrupted time-series design is another common and useful method of evaluating the effectiveness of crime prevention programmes (see, for example, the evaluation of saturation patrols in Nashville by Boydstun (1975)). Time series evaluations are typically used in evaluations of crime prevention programmes in which changes in crime rates over time are recorded. The simplest version of this method is to plot say monthly crime rates for a period of one or two years before an intervention programme and for a similar period after the programme has been implemented. The clearest outcome occurs when the time series changes in a favourable direction at the time of the introduction of the intervention and in an unfavourable direction at the time of its withdrawal. The design can be strengthened by including an untreated control group, which helps control for 'history' (natural changes among the two groups), but other methods need to be used to control for 'local history' (affecting just one of the groups).

4.6.3   Evaluation is technically complicated and conceptually fraught with difficulties (see Ekblom and Pease, in press). The degree of uncertainty will vary, but in all cases, even with random experiments, the scope for failure is significant. In practice, many evaluations to date of crime prevention initiatives have been either over-simplistic and/or seriously flawed. Many have failed to differentiate the independent effects of individual measures in multi-component initiatives and frequently no proof is provided which could confirm that any observed reduction in crime was caused by the initiative. If the technical and financial resources for a rigorous evaluation are not available or forthcoming, it may be preferable to forego evaluation altogether; poor evaluations may only produce misinformation.

4.6.4   Evaluations can be time-consuming, disruptive, costly and may be even threatening. Research can expose deficiencies in management or unethical practices. Sometimes political and/or financial pressure to illustrate the effectiveness of an initiative can overrule the need for objective results. However, researchers and practitioners can both benefit from collaboration, even though they may have different priorities and interests. Practitioners can help researchers to remain grounded and can apply a degree of healthy scepticism to the validity and certainty of findings. And they can help to put the success or failure of an initiative into a cost-related perspective. Evaluation need not be seen as a purely technical and scientific process and practitioners can play an important part in providing a necessary context for the research; indeed in some cases assessments by practitioners of changes that have been made, may usefully complement the more precise measurements made by independent evaluators.

APPENDIX I. LIST OF CRIME PREVENTION INITIATIVES

CHAPTER 2.   Page

CHAPTER 3.   **Page**

CHAPTER 4.   **Page**

ALBRECHT, H.J. and KALMHOUT, A. (1990) Drug Policies in Western Europe. Freiburg i. Breisgau: Max Planck Institut fuer Ausländisches und Internationales Strafrecht.

ASSOCIATION OF CHIEF PROBATION OFFICERS, (1993) 'Social Circumstances of Younger Offenders under Supervision'. Research report. Lancaster: Lancaster University.

ATKINS, S., HUSAIN, S. and STOREY, A. (1991) The Influence of Street Lighting on Crime and Fear of Crime. Crime Prevention Unit Paper No. 28. London: Home Office.

AUSTIN, C. (1988) The Prevention of Robbery at Building Society Branches. Crime Prevention Unit Paper No.14. London: Home Office.

BALDWIN, J. and BOTTOMS, A. E. (1976). The Urban Criminal: A Study in Sheffield. London: Tavistock Publication.

BARNUM, R. (1987) 'Biomedical problems in juvenile delinquency: Issues in diagnosis and treatment.' In: Wilson, J.Q. and Loury, G.C. (eds.) Families, schools and delinquency prevention, vol. III of 'From Children to Citizens'. New York: Springer Verlag.

BARR, R. and PEASE, K. (1990) 'Crime placement, displacement and deflection'. In: M. Tonry and N. Morris (Eds.) Crime and Justice: A Review of Research. Vol.12. Chicago: University of Chicago Press.

BEAVON, D. J. K , BRANTINGHAM, P and BRANTINGHAM, P (1994) 'The influence of street networks on the patterning of property offenses'. In: R. V. Clarke (ed.) Crime Prevention Studies Volume 2 Monsey, NY : Criminal Justice Press.

BECKETT, I. and HART, J. (1981) Neighbourhood Policing: A system and behavioural study of police operations in the urban environment. The City University. London: Unpublished B.Sc. dissertation.

BELLKNAP, J. (1989) 'The Economics-Crime Link'. Criminal Justice Abstracts 21, 1, pp 140-157.

BENNETT, T.H. (1989) 'Factors Related to Participation in Neighbourhood Watch Schemes', British Journal of Criminology, Vol.29, No.3 pp. 207-218.

BENNETT, T.H. (1990) Evaluating Neighbourhood Watch. Aldershot: Gower.

BENNETT, T.H. and LUPTON, R. (1992a) A National Survey of the Organisation and Use of Community Constables, British Journal of Criminology, 32, 2, 167-182.

BENNETT, T.H. and LUPTON, R. (1992b) 'A National Activity Survey of Police Work'. The Howard Journal of Criminal Justice, vol. 31, no. 3, pp 200-223.

BENNETT, T.H. and KEMP, C. (1994) An Evaluation of Sector-Based Problem-Oriented Policing in Thames Valley Police Force Area. Report to the Home Office Research and Planning Unit. Cambridge: Institute of Criminology.

BENNETT, T.W. and WRIGHT, R. (1984) Burglars on Burglary: Prevention and the Offender. Farnborough: Gower.

BESHAROV, D.J. (1987) 'Giving the juvenile court a preschool education.' In Wilson, J.Q. and Loury, G.C. (eds.) Families, schools and delinquency prevention, vol. III of 'From Children to Citizens'. New York: Springer Verlag.

BEVILLE, S.L. and NICKERSON, C. (1981) Improving the Quality of Youth Work: A Strategy for Delinquency Prevention. Washington D.C.: U.S. Department of Justice.

BOTTOMS, A.E. (1993) 'Crime and Insecurity in the City'. Paper presented at a conference in Belgium.

BOTTOMS, A.E. and XANTHOS, P (1981) 'Housing Policy and Crime in the British public Sector'. In: BRANTINGHAM, P.L. and BRANTINGHAM, P.J. (eds) Environmental Criminology Beverly Hills: Sage.

BOTTOMS, A.E., MAWBY R.I. and WALKER, M. (1987) 'A localised crime survey in contrasting areas of a city'. British Journal of Criminology, vol.27, pp 125-154.

BOTTOMS, A.E. and WILES, P. (1988) 'Crime and housing policy: a framework for crime prevention analysis', in: T. Hope and M. Shaw (eds.) Communities and Crime Reduction. London: HMSO.

BOTTOMS, A.E. and WILES, P. (1994) 'Understanding Crime Prevention in Late Modern Societies'. Paper presented at the 22nd Cropwood Conference, University of Cambridge, September 1994.

BOX, S. (1987) Recession, Crime and Punishment. London: Macmillan.

BOYDSTUN, J.E. (1975) San Diego Field Interrogation: Final Report, Police Foundation, Washington D.C.

BRANTINGHAM, T.J. and BRANTINGHAM, P.L (1993) 'Environment, Routine, and Situation: Toward a Pattern Theory of Crime'. In: CLARKE, R.V.G. and FELSON, M. (eds) Routine Activity and Rational Choice. Advances in Criminological Theory. Volume 5. London: Transaction Books.

BRANTINGHAM, P.J. and FAUST, F.L. (1976) 'A conceptual model of crime prevention.' Crime and Delinquency, no.22, (July).

BRIGHT, J. (1992) Crime Prevention in America: A British Perspective. Reading: Office of International Criminal Justice.

BRIGHT, J., MALONEY, H., PETTERSSEN, G. and FARR, J. (1985) After Entryphones: Improving Management and Security in Multi-Story Blocks. London: Safe Neighbourhoods Unit.

BUCK, A.J. and HAKIM, S. (1993) 'Burglar alarms and the choice behaviour of burglars: a suburban phenomenon', Journal of Criminal Justice, Vol.21, pp.497-507.

BULLOCK, R., LITTLE, M. and MILLHAM, S. (1993) Residential Care for Children: A Review of Research. London: HMSO

BURBIDGE, M. (1984) 'British public housing and crime: a review'. In: R. Clarke and T. Hope. (Eds.) Coping with Burglary. Boston, MA.: Kluwer-Nijhoff.

BURROWS, J. (1980. 'Closed circuit television and crime on the London Underground'. In: Clarke, R.V.G. and Mayhew, P. (eds.), Designing out Crime. London: HMSO.

CAMPBELL, D. and TRAVIS, A. (1994) 'Crackdown urged on 'cowboy' security firms', The Guardian, 18 August, London: Guardian Newspapers Ltd.

CANADIAN COUNCIL ON CHILDREN AND YOUTH, (1989) 'Safer tomorrows begin today: Promoting safer, healthier communities through early investment in children.' Ottawa.

CAPOWICH, G.E. and ROEHL, J.A. (1994) 'Problem-oriented Policing: actions and effectiveness in San Diego'. In: ROSENBAUM, D. (ed) The Challenge of Community Policing: Testing the Promises. London: Sage.

CARR, K and SPRING, G. (1993) 'Public transport and safety: A community right and a community responsibility' In: R. V. Clarke (ed.) Crime Prevention Studies Volume 2. Monsey, NY: Criminal Justice Press.

CIREL, P., EVANS, P., McGILLIS, D. and WHITCOMB, D. (1977) Community Crime Prevention, Seattle, Washington: An Exemplary Project. U.S. Department of Justice. Washington, D.C.: Government Printing Office.

CLARKE, R.V.G. (1980) 'Situational crime prevention: theory and practice', British Journal of Criminology, Vol.20, pp.136-147.

CLARKE, R.V.G. (1983) 'Situational crime prevention: its theoretical basis and practical scope', in: M. Tonry and N. Morris (eds.) Crime and Justice: An Annual Review of Research, Vol. 4., Chicago: University of Chicago Press.

CLARKE, R.V.G. (ed) (1992) Situational Crime Prevention: Successful Case Studies. New York: Harrow and Heston.

CLARKE, R.V.G. (1993) 'Fare evasion and automatic ticket collection on the London Underground' In: R. V. Clarke Crime prevention Studies Volume 1. Monsey, NY: Criminal Justice Press.

CLARKE, R.V.G. and HOUGH, J.M. (1984) Crime and Police Effectiveness. Home Office Study No. 79. London: HMSO.

CLARKE, R.V.G. and MAYHEW, P. (1988) 'The British gas suicide story and its criminological implications'. In: M. Tonry and N. Morris (Eds.) Crime and Justice: An Annual Review of Research. Volume 10. Chicago: University of Chicago Press. (Source: Clarke, 1992).

COHEN, L.E., and FELSON, M. (1979) 'Social change and crime rate trends: a routine activity approach', American Sociological Review, 44. pp. 588-608.

COLDER, J.K. (1987) 'Petty crime control in shopping centres.' Interim report. Den Hague: WODC, Ministry of Justice.

COOK, P. J (1982) 'The Role of Firearms in Violent Crime' In: M. E Wolfgang and N. A Weimer (ed.) Criminal Violence Beverly Hills: C. A : Sage.

COOK, T.D. and CAMPBELL, D.T. (1979) Quasi-Experimentation: Design and Analysis Issues for Field Settings. Chicago: Rand McNally.

CORNISH, D.B. and CLARKE, R.V.G. (1988) 'Situational Prevention, displacement of crime and rational choice theory'. In: HEAL, K. and LAYCOCK, G. (eds) Situational Crime Prevention: From theory into practice. London: HMSO.

CROMWELL, P.F., OLSON, J.N., and AVARY, D. (1991) Breaking and Entering: An Ethnographic Analysis of Burglary. Newbury Park, CA: Sage.

CURRIE, E. (1988) 'Two visions of community crime prevention.' In: Hope, T. and Shaw, M. (eds.). Communities and Crime Reduction. London: HMSO.

CURRIE, E. (1993) Reckoning: Drugs, the Cities and the American Future. New York: Hill and Wang.

DESCHAMPS, S., BRANTINGHAM, P.L. and BRANTINGHAM, P.J. (1991) 'The British Colombia Transit Fare Evasion Audit: A description of a situation prevention process'. Security journal, vol. 2, pp 211-218.

DOIG, B. and LITTLEWOOD, J. (1992) Policy Evaluation: The Role of Social Research. London: Department of the Environment.

DRYFOOS, J.G. (1990) Adolescents at risk. New York: Oxford University Press.

ECK, J.E. (1993) 'The threat of crime displacement', Criminal Justice Abstracts, September, pp.527-546.

ECK, J.E. and SPELMAN, W. (1987) 'Who ya gonna call? The police as problem busters.' Crime and Delinquency, vol.33, no.1, pp 31-52.

EKBLOM, P. (1979) 'Police truancy patrols'. In: Burrows, J., Ekblom, P. and Heal, K. (1979) Crime Prevention and the Police. Home Office Research Study No.55. London: HMSO.

EKBLOM, P. (1986) 'The Prevention of Shop Theft: an approach through crime analysis'. Crime Prevention Unit Paper No. 5. London: Home Office Crime Prevention Unit.

EKBLOM, P. (1987) Preventing Robberies at Sub-Post Offices: An Evaluation of a Security Initiative. Crime Prevention Unit Paper No.9. London: Home Office.

EKBLOM, P. (1988) 'Getting the Best out of Crime Analysis.' Crime Prevention Unit Paper No. 10. London: Home Office Crime Prevention Unit.

EKBLOM, P. (1994) 'Proximal circumstances: a mechanism-based classification of crime prevention', Crime Prevention Studies, Vol.2., pp.185-232.

EKBLOM, P. and PEASE, K. (in press) 'Evaluating Crime Prevention'. In: TONRY, M. and FARRINGTON, D.F. (eds) Building a Safer Society: Strategic Approaches to Crime Prevention. Crime and Justice 19. Chicago: University of Chicago Press.

FARRELL, G. (1992) 'Multiple victimisation: its extent and significance'. International Review of Victimology, vol. 2, pp 85-102.

FARRELL, G. and PEASE, K. (1993) Once Bitten, Twice Bitten: Repeat Victimisation and its Implications for Crime Prevention. Crime Prevention Unit Paper 46. London: Home Office.

FARRINGTON, D. (1993) 'Understanding and Preventing Bullying'. In: Tonry, M. (ed) Crime and Justice. vol. 17. University of Chicago Press.

FARRINGTON, D.P. (1994) 'Human Development and Criminal Careers' In: Maguire, M. Morgan, R. and Reiner, R. The Oxford Handbook of Criminology. Oxford: Clarendon Press.

FARRINGTON, D.P., GALLAGHER, B., MORLEY, L., St. LEDGER, R.J. and WEST, D.J. (1986) 'Unemployment, School Leaving and Crime'. British Journal of Criminology vol. 26, no. 4, pp 335-356.

FARRINGTON, D.P., BOWEN. S., BUCKLE, A., BURNS-HOWELL, J., BURROWS, J. and SPEED, M. (1993) 'An experiment on the prevention of shoplifting' In: R. V. Clarke Crime prevention Studies Volume 1 Monsey, NY: Criminal Justice Press.

FENNELLY, L. J. (1982) 'How to Conduct Security Surveys'. In: FENNELLY, L. J. (ed) Handbook of Loss Prevention and Crime Prevention Boston: Butterworths.

FIENBERG, S.E., LARANTZ, K and REISS, A.J. (1974) 'Redesigning the Kansas City Preventive Patrol Experiment'. In: HALLECK, S.L. (ed) The Aldine Criminal Justice Annual Chicago: Aldine.

FINESTONE, H. (1976) Victims of Change, Westport: Greenwood Press.

FLEMING, R. and BURROWS, J. (1987) The Case for Lighting as a Means of Preventing Crime. Home Office Research and Planning Unit.

FORRESTER, D., CHATTERTON, M. and PEASE, K. (1988) The Kirkholt Burglary Prevention Project, Rochdale. Crime Prevention Unit: Paper 13. London: Home Office.

FOSTER, J. and HOPE, T. (1993) 'Housing, Community and Crime: The Impact of the Priority Estates Project.' Home Office Research Study No. 131. London: HMSO.

FOWLER, F.J., McCALLA, M.E. and MANGIONE, T.W. (1979) Reducing Residential Crime and Fear: The Hartford Neighbourhood Crime Prevention Program. Washington D.C.: US Government Printing Office.

GABOR, T. (1990) 'Crime displacement and situational prevention: towards the development of some principles'. Canadian Journal of Criminology, Vol.32, No.1, pp.41-73.

GAROFALO, J. and McLEOD, M. (1988). 'Improving the use and effectiveness of Neighbourhood Watch programs.' Report prepared for the National Institute of Justice, US Department of Justice.

GIBBON, J. and THORPE, S. (1990) 'Can Voluntary Support Projects Help Vulnerable Families? The Work of Home-Start'. British Journal of Social Work. 19, pp. 189-202.

GOLDSTEIN, H. (1987) 'Toward community-oriented policing: potential, basic requirements, and threshold questions.' Crime and Delinquency, vol.33, no.1, pp 6-30.

GOLDSTEIN, H. (1990) Problem-Oriented Policing. London: McGraw-Hill.

GOTTFREDSON, D.C. and GOTTFREDSON, G.D. (1986) 'The school action effectiveness study.' Final report. Baltimore: John Hopkins University.

GRAHAM, J. (1988a) 'Families, Parenting and Delinquency Prevention'. Research Bulletin, No. 26 London: Home Office.

GRAHAM, J. (1988b) 'Schools, Disruptive Behaviour and Delinquency'. Home Office Research Study, No. 96. London: HMSO.

GRAHAM, J. (1988c) 'Crime prevention in the Federal Republic of Germany.' In: Graham, J. (ed.) Research Bulletin: Special European Edition, Home Office Research and Planning Unit, No. 24. London: HMSO.

GRAHAM, J. (1992) 'The School'. In: Family, school and community: towards a social crime prevention agenda. Swindon: Crime Concern.

GRAHAM, J. (1993 'Crime Prevention Policies in Europe'. European Journal of Criminal Law and Criminal Justice, vol. 1, issue 2, pp 126 - 142.

GRAHAM, J. and SMITH, D. (1993) Diversion From Offending: the Role of the Youth Service. Swindon: Crime Concern.

GRAHAM, J. and UTTING, D. (1994) 'Families, Schools and Criminality Prevention'. Paper presented at the 22nd Cropwood Conference, University of Cambridge, September 1994.

GREENBERG, S.W., ROHE, W.M. and WILLIAMS, J.R. (1985) Informal Citizen Action and Crime Prevention at the Neighbourhood Level. U.S. Department of Justice. Washington, D.C.: Government Printing Office.

HANNON, P., WEINBERGER, J. and NUTBROWN,C. (1991) 'A Study of Work with Parents to Promote Early Literacy Development'. Research papers in education. vol.6, no.2, pp. 77-97.

HAWKINS, J.D. and LISHNER, D.M. (1983) Cooperating to Prevent Delinquency: A School Based Approach. Seattle: Social Development Research Group, University of Washington.

HELLER, N.B., STENZEL, W.W., GILL, A.D., KOLDE, R.A., and SCHIMERMAN, S.R. (1975) Operation Identification Projects: An Assessment of Effectiveness. National Evaluation Program, Phase 1, Summary Report. Washington, D.C.: National Institute for Law Enforcement and Criminal Justice.

HILL, N. (1986) 'Prepayment coin meters: a target for burglary'. Crime Prevention Unit Paper No. 6. London: Home Office Crime Prevention Unit.

HILL, R.B. (1985) 'Foster care and delinquency.' Research report for the National Institute for Juvenile Justice and Delinquency Prevention. Washington D.C.

HOARE, M.A., STEWART, G. and PURCELL, C.M. (1984) 'The problem-oriented approach: Four pilot studies.' London: Metropolitan Police Management Services Division.

HOME OFFICE, (1990) Partnership in crime prevention. London: HMSO.

HOPE, T. (1985) 'Implementing Crime Prevention Measures.' Home Office Research Study No. 86, London: HMSO.

HOPE, T. (1986) 'Council tenants and crime'. Research Bulletin No. 21. London: Home Office Research and Planning Unit.

HOPE, T. (1988) 'Support for Neighbourhood Watch: a British Crime Survey analysis'. In Communities and Crime Reduction, ed. by. T. Hope and M. Shaw: London: HMSO. Pp. 146-161.

HOPE, T. (1994) 'Community Crime Prevention'. In. Farrington, D.P. and Tonry, M. Crime and Justice. Volume 19. Chicago: University of Chicago Press.

HOPE, T. and SHAW, M. (1988) 'Community approaches to reducing crime.' In: HOPE, T. and SHAW. M. (eds.). Communities and Crime Reduction. London: HMSO.

HOPE, T. and FOSTER, J. (1992) 'Conflicting forces: changing the dynamics of crime and community on a 'problem' estate' British Journal of Criminology. Vol.32, pp.488-504.

HOUGH, M., CLARKE, R.V.G. and MAYHEW, P. (1980) 'Introduction.' In: CLARKE, R.V.G. and MAYHEW, P. (eds.). Designing out Crime. London: HMSO.

HUNTER, R.D. and JEFFERY, C.R. (1992) 'Preventing convenience store robbery through environmental design'. In: R.V.G. Clarke (Ed.) Situational Crime Prevention: Successful Case Studies. New York: Harrow and Heston.

HUSAIN, S. (1988) 'Neighbourhood Watch in England and Wales: a locational analysis.' Crime Prevention Unit Paper No. 12. London: Home Office Crime Prevention Unit.

IRVING, B., BIRD, C., HIBBERD, M. and WILLMORE, J. (1989) Neighbourhood Policing: The Natural History of a Policing Experiment. London: The Police Foundation.

INTERNATIONAL TRAINING, RESEARCH AND EVALUATION COUNCIL (1977) National Evaluation Program Phase 1 Summary Report: Crime Prevention Surveys. Washington, D.C., National Institute of Law Enforcement and Criminal Justice.

JEFFERY, C.R. (1977) Crime Prevention Through Environmental Design. London: Sage.

JENSEN, L. (1988) 'Crime prevention in Denmark'. In: GRAHAM, J. (ed) Home Office Research Bulletin: Special European Edition. London: Home Office.

JUDD, C.M. and KENNY, D.A. (1981) Estimating the Effects of Social Interventions. Cambridge: Cambridge University Press.

JUNGER-TAS, J. (1988) 'Crime prevention in the Netherlands.' In: Graham.J. (ed.) Research Bulletin: Special European Edition, Home Office Research and Planning Unit, No. 24. London: HMSO.

KAISER, G. (1988. Kriminologie: Ein Lehrbuch. Heidelberg: C.F.Mueller Juristischer Verlag.

KALLE, E. (1987) 'The prevention of urban violence and insecurity in post-war housing: The case of Geeren-Noord, Breda.' In: Council of Europe, Urban violence and insecurity: the role of local authorities. Strasbourg: Proceedings of International conference.

KATONA, G. (1994) Survey on Crime Prevention in Europe. RTF Institute for Police Management Training and Research. Budapest: National Police Headquarters.

KAZDIN, A.E. (1993) 'Treatment of Conduct Disorder: progress and directions in psychotherapy research'. Development and Psychopathology. 5, pp. 277-310.

KELLAM, S.G. and REBOK, G.W. (1992) 'Building Developmental and Etiological Theory through Epidemiologically Based Intervention Trials'. In: McCord, J. and Tremblay, R.E. (eds) 'Preventing Anti-social Behaviour: Interventions from Birth through Adolescence.' New York: Guildford Press.

KELLING, G.L., PATE, T., DIECKMAN, D. and BROWN, C.E. (1974) 'The Kansas City preventive patrol experiment.' A technical report. Washington D.C.: Police Foundation.

KELLING, G.L., EDWARDS, S.M., and MOORE, M.H. (1986) 'Federally funded community crime control: Urban initiatives anti-crime program.' Criminal Justice Policy Review, vol.1, no.1, pp 58-75.

KING, M. (1988) 'How to make social crime prevention work: The French experience.' Occasional Paper. London: NACRO

KOBRIN, S. (1959) 'The Chicago Area Project-A 25 year assessment'. The Annals of the American Academy, Vol.322, pp.19-29.

KOCH, I. (1988) 'SSP - Det social sympatiske politi.' Social Kritik, no.1, pp 8-21.

KOLVIN, I., MILLER, F.J.W. SCOTT, D.M. GATZANIS, S.R.M. and FLEETING, M.(1990) Continuities Of Deprivation? The Newcastle 1000 Family Study. Aldershot: Avebury.

KOPER, C.S. (1992) Analysis of Short-term Deterrent Effects of patrol Car Presence in Hot Spots. Washington D.C.: Crime Control Institute.

KRIKORIAN, G. (1986) 'Prevention as a strategy for combatting urban crime: theoretical considerations and their application to local situation in France'. International Criminal Police Review, no. 396, pp 71-80.

LALLY, J.R., MANGIONE, P.L., HONIG, A.S. and WITTNER, D.S. (1988) 'More Pride, Less Delinquency: Findings from the ten year follow-up study of the Syracuse University Family Development Research Program'. Zero-to-three, vol. 8, no. 4, pp 13-18.

LARSON, R.C. (1976) 'What Happened to Patrol Operations in Kansas City?' Journal of Criminal Justice. Vol.3, pp. 267-297.

LAYCOCK, G. (1985) 'Property Marking: A Deterrent to Domestic Burglary?' Crime Prevention Unit Paper no. 3. London: Home Office.

LAYCOCK, G. (1989) 'An Evaluation of Domestic Security Surveys'. Crime Prevention Unit Paper no. 18. London: Home Office

LAYCOCK, G. (1991) 'Operation Identification, or the Power of Publicity?' Security Journal, vol. 2, no. 2, pp 67-72.

LAYCOCK, G. and TILLEY, N. (forthcoming) 'Policing and Neighbourhood Watch: Strategic Issues'. Crime Prevention and Detection Series, no. XX. London: Home Office Police Research Group.

LENKOWSKI, L. (1987) 'The Federal Government and the Family.' In: Wilson, J.Q. and Loury, G.C. (eds.) Families, schools and delinquency prevention, vol. III of 'From Children to Citizens'. New York: Springer Verlag.

LESTER, D. (1993) 'Controlling crime facilitators: evidence from research on homicide and suicide'. In: In: R.V.Clarke (Ed.) Crime Prevention Studies Volume 1. New York: Criminal Justice Press.

LINDEN, R. and MINCH, C. (1985) 'Rural crime prevention in Canada.' Working Paper. Ottawa: Ministry of the Solicitor General.

LITTON, R.A. and PEASE, K. (1984) 'Crimes and claims: the case of burglary insurance'. In, Clarke, R.V.G. and Hope, T. (eds.), Coping with Burglary. Boston: Kluwer-Nijhoff.

LOEBER, R. (1987) 'What policy makers and practitioners can learn from family studies of juvenile conduct problems and delinquency.' In: Wilson, J.Q. and Loury, G.C. (eds.) Families, schools and delinquency prevention, vol. III of 'From Children to Citizens'. New York: Springer Verlag.

LOEBER, R. and DISHION, T.J. (1983) 'Early predictors of male delinquency: a review.' In Wilson, J.Q. and Loury, G.C. (eds.) Families, schools and delinquency prevention, vol. III of 'From Children to Citizens'. New York: Springer Verlag.

LOEBER, R. and STOUTHAMER-LOEBER, M. (1986) 'Family Factors As Correlates And Predictors Of Juvenile Conduct Problems And Delinquency'. In: Tonry, M. And Morris, N. (Eds): Crime And Justice-An Annual Review Of Research. vol.7. Chicago: University Of Chicago.

LOHMAN, P.M.S. and VAN DIJK, A.G. (1988) 'Neighbourhood watch in the Netherlands.' The Hague: National Crime Prevention Bureau.

LOURY, G.C. (1987) 'The family as context for delinquency prevention: demographic trends and political realities.' In Wilson, J.Q. and Loury, G.C. (eds.) Families, schools and delinquency prevention, vol. III of 'From Children to Citizens'. New York: Springer Verlag.

LURIGIO, A.J. and ROSENBAUM, D. (1986) 'Evaluation research in community crime prevention: a critical look at the field'. In: Rosenbaum, D.P. (Ed.). Community Crime Prevention: Does It Work? London: Sage.

MALINOWSKY-RUMMELL, R. and HANSEN, D.J. (1993) 'Long-Term Consequences of Childhood Physical Abuse'. Psychological Bulletin. 114, pp. 68-79.

MARTINSON, R. (1974) 'What works? - Questions and answers about prison reform.' The Public Interest, (Spring), pp 22-52.

MATTHEWS, R. (1992) 'Kerb-Crawling, Prostitution and Multi-Agency Policing'. Crime Prevention Unit Paper, no. 43. London: Home Office

MATZA, D. (1964) Delinquency and Drift. New York: Wiley.

MAYHEW, P. (1976) The Effectiveness of Street Lighting in Preventing Crime. Unpublished report by the Home Office Research Unit. Cited in: Fleming, R. and Burrows, J. (1987) The Case for Lighting as a Means of Preventing Crime, Home Office Research and Planning Unit.

MAYHEW, P. (1984). 'Target-hardening: how much of an answer?'. In: Clarke, R.V.G. and Hope, T. (eds.), Coping with Burglary. Boston: Kluwer-Nijhoff.

MAYHEW, P., CLARKE, R.V.G., STURMAN, A., and HOUGH, J.M. (1976) Crime as Opportunity. Home Office Research Study No. 34. London.

MAYHEW, P., CLARKE, R.V.G., BURROWS, J.N., HOUGH, J.M., and WINCHESTER, S.W.C. (1979) Crime in Public View. Home Office Research Study No.49. London: HMSO.

MAYHEW, P., CLARKE, R.V.G., BURROWS, J.N., HOUGH, J.M., and WINCHESTER, S.W.C. (1980). 'Natural surveillance and vandalism to telephone kiosks'. In: Clarke, R.V.G. and Mayhew, P. (eds.), Designing out Crime. London: HMSO.

MAYHEW, P., ELLIOT, P. and DOWDS, L. (1989) 'The 1988 British Crime Survey', Home Office Research Study, No. 111. London: HMSO.

MAYHEW, P. MAUNG, A. N and MIRRLEES-BLACK, C. (1993) The 1992 British Crime Survey. HORS 132. London HMSO.

McALLISTER, D. LEITCH, S. and PAYNE, D. (1993) Crime Prevention and Housebreaking in Scotland: Findings from the 1989 and 1990 Labour Force Survey. Scottish Office Central Research Unit Paper Edinburgh'. Scottish Office.

McGAHEY, R.M. (1986) 'Economic conditions, neighbourhood organization and urban crime.' In: Tonry, M. and Morris, N. (eds.). Crime and Justice, vol.9. Chicago: University of Chicago Press.

McINNES, P. and BURGESS, G. (1984) 'The environmental design and management approach to crime prevention in residential environments.' Research Report. Ottawa: Ministry of the Solicitor General.

MEREDITH, C. (1988) 'Apartment crime prevention demonstration project.' Research Report. Ottawa: Ministry of the Solicitor General.

MOORE, C. and BROWN, J. (1981) Community Versus Crime. Dorchester: Bedford Square Press.

MORTIMORE, P. and MORTIMORE, J. (1984) 'Parents and School in Education'. Education. 5, October 1984.

MORTIMORE, P., SAMMONS, P., STOLL, L., LEWIS, D. and ECOB, R. (1988) School Matters: The Junior Years. Shepton Mallett: Open Books.

MUSHENO, M.C., LEVINE, J.P. and PALUMO, D.J. (1978) 'Television surveillance and crime prevention: evaluating an attempt to create defensible space in public housing', Social Science Quarterly, Vol.58, March, pp. 647-656.

MVA CONSULTANCY, (1991) Links Between Truancy And Delinquency. Report Prepared For The Scottish Office Education Department. Edinburgh.

NATIONAL CRIME PREVENTION COUNCIL, (1986) 'Preventing crime in urban communities.' Washington D.C.: NCPC.

NEWMAN, O. (1972) Defensible Space: Crime Prevention through Urban Design. New York: MacMillan.

NEWMAN, O. and FRANCK, K.A. (1980) 'Factors influencing crime and instability in urban housing developments.' Executive Summary. National Institute of Justice. Washington, DC: Government Printing Office.
NUTTALL, C.P. (1988) 'Crime prevention in Canada.' In: Hope, T. and Shaw, M. (eds.). Communities and Crime Reduction. London: HMSO.

O'DONNELL, C.R., LYDGATE, T. and FO, W. (1979) 'The Buddy system: review and follow-up'. Child Behaviour Therapy, no.1, pp 161-169.

OFFICE OF JUVENILE JUSTICE AND DELINQUENCY PREVENTION. (1981) Delinquency Prevention: Theories and Strategies. Washington D.C.: Ministry of Justice.

O'KEEFE, J.D. and MENDELSOHN, H. (1984) Taking a Bite out of Crime: the impact of a mass media crime prevention campaign Washington D.C.: National Institute of Justice.

OLWEUS, D. (1991) 'Bully/victim problems among school children: Basic facts and effects of a school based intervention program'. In: RUBIN, K. and PEPLER, D. (eds) The Development and Treatment of Childhood Aggression. Hillsdale: Erlbaum.

OSBORN, S. (1992) Review of Housing-Related Crime Prevention. London: Department of the Environment.

OSBORN, S. (1993) Housing Safe Communities. Safe Neighbourhoods Unit. London: HMSO.

OSBORN, S. and WEST, D.J. (1978) 'Effectiveness of Various Predictors of Criminal Careers'. Journal of Adolescence 1, pp 101-117.

OSBORN, S. and BRIGHT, J. (1989) 'Crime prevention and community safety: A practical guide for local authorities.' London: NACRO, Safe Neighbourhoods Unit.

PAINTER, K. (1988) Lighting and Crime Prevention: The Edmonton Project. London: Middlesex Polytechnic.

PAPWORTH, G. (1994) 'Locks a key issue in burglary claims', The Guardian, 13 August, London: Guardian Newspapers Ltd.

PATE, A., WYCOFF, M.A., SKOGAN, W. and SHERMAN, L.W. (1986) Reducing Fear of Crime in Houston and Newark: A Summary Report. Washington D.C.: Police Foundation.

PATTERSON, G.R. (1994) 'Some Characteristics of a Developmental Theory for Early Onset Delinquency'. In: HAUGAARD, J.J. and LENZENWEGER, M.F. (eds) 'Frontiers of Developmental Psychopathology'. Oxford University Press.

PATTERSON, G.R., CHAMBERLAIN, P. and REID, J.B. (1982) 'A comparative evaluation of a parent training program.' Behaviour Therapy, vol.13, pp 638-650.

PAWSON, R. and TILLEY, N. (1992) 'Re-evaluation: rethinking research on corrections and crime'. Yearbook on Correctional Education. pp 19 - 49.

PAWSON, R. and TILLEY, N. (1994) 'What works in evaluation research?' British Journal of Criminology, vol. 34. pp 291 306.

PENNELL, S., CURTIS, C. and HENDERSON, J. (1986) Guardian Angels: An Assessment of Citizen Response to Crime. National Institute of Justice. U.S. Department of Justice. Washington D.C.: Government Printing Office.

PENNELL, S., CURTIS, C., HENDERSON, J. and TAYMAN, J. (1989) 'Guardian angels, a unique approach to crime prevention', Crime and Delinquency, Vol.35, No.3, pp.378-400.

POLVI, N., LOOMAN, T., HUMPHRIES, C. and PEASE, K. (1990) 'Repeat break-and-enter victimisations: time course and crime prevention opportunity', Journal of Police Science and Administration, Vol.17, pp.8-11.

POLVI, N., LOOMAN, T., HUMPHRIES, C. and PEASE, K. (1991) 'The time course of repeat burglary victimisation', British Journal of Criminology, Vol.31, pp.411-414.

POWER, A. (1988) 'Housing, Poverty and Crime.' In: DOWNES, D. (ed). Crime and the City. London: Macmillan.

POYNER, B. and WEBB, B. (1987) Successful Crime Prevention Case Studies. London: Tavistock Institute of Human Relations. Document No. 2T 563.

POYNER, B. (1988) 'Video cameras and bus vandalism', Security Administration, Vol.11, pp.44-51.

PRANSKY, J. (1991) Prevention: The Critical Need. Burrell Foundation, Springfield: Paradigm Press.

REID, J.B. (1993) 'Prevention Of Conduct Disorder Before And After School Entry: Relating Interventions To Developmental Findings'. Development and Psychopathology. 5, pp. 243-262.

REID, J.B., EDDY, M., BANK, L. and FETROW, R. (1994) 'A Universal Prevention Strategy For Conduct Disorder: Some Preliminary Findings'. Paper Presented To SRCAP Conference, June 1994, London.

REPPETTO, T. (1976) 'Crime prevention and the displacement phenomenon', Crime and Delinquency, Vol.22, pp.166-177.

RILEY, D. and SHAW, M. (1985). 'Parental Supervision and Juvenile Delinquency.' Home Office Research Study No. 83. London: HMSO.

ROCK, P. (1988) 'Crime reduction initiatives on problem estates.' In: Hope, T. and Shaw, M. (eds.). Communities and Crime Reduction. London: HMSO.

ROSENBAUM, D. (1986) Community Crime Prevention: Does it Work? London: Sage.

ROSENBAUM, D. (1988) 'Community crime prevention: a review and synthesis of the literature'. Justice Quarterly, vol.5, pp 323-395.

ROSENBAUM, D.P., LEWIS, D.A. and GRANT, J.A. (1985) The Impact of Community Crime Prevention Programs in Chicago: Can Neighbourhood Organization Make a Difference? Final Report. Volume One. Illinois: Northwestern University. Center for Urban Affairs and Policy Research.

RUTTER, M., MAUGHAN, B., MORTIMORE, P. and OUSTON, J. (1979) Fifteen Thousand Hours: Secondary Schools and their Effects on Children. London: Open Books.

RUTTER, M. and GILLER, H. (1983) Juvenile Delinquency: Trends and Perspectives. London: Penguin.

RUTTER, M., QUINTON, D. and LIDDLE, C. (1983) 'Parenting in two generations: Looking backwards and looking forwards.' In MADGE, N. (ed.) Families at risk. London: Heinemann.

SAMPSON, A. and PHILLIPS, C. (1992) Multiple Victimisation: Racial Attacks on an East London Estate. Crime Prevention Unit Series Paper 36. London: Home Office.

SARNECKI, J. (1992) 'The State of Knowledge in Sweden'. In: ROBERT, P. (ed) Crime Prevention Policies: A Scientific Assessment. Paris:CESDIP.

SCHWARTZ, A.L. and CLARREN, S.N. (1977) The Cincinnati Team Policing Experiment: A Summary Report. Police Foundation, Washington D.C.

SCHWEINHART, L.J. (1987) 'Can preschool programs help prevent delinquency?' In Wilson, J.Q. and Loury, G.C. (eds.) Families, schools and delinquency prevention, vol. III of 'From Children to Citizens'. New York: Springer Verlag.

SCHWEINHART, L.J. and WEIKART, D.P.(1993) A Summary of Significant Benefits: the High/Scope Perry Pre-school Study through age 27. High/Scope Press: Ypsilanti/Michigan.

SEITZ, V., ROSENBAUM, L.K. and APFEL, N.H. (1985) 'Effects of family support intervention: A ten year follow-up.' Child Development, vol.56, pp 376-391.

SHAPLAND, J., WILES, P. and WILCOX, P. (1994) Targeted Crime Reduction: Principles and Methods. London: Police Research Group.

SHAW, C.R. and McKAY, H.D. (1942) Juvenile delinquency and urban areas. Chicago: University of Chicago Press.

SHERMAN, L.W. (1992) 'Policing and Crime Control'. In: Modern Policing: Crime and Justice, vol. 15. Chicago: University of Chicago Press.

SHERMAN, L.W., GARTIN, P.R., and BUERGER, M.E. (1989) 'Hot spots of predatory crime: routine activities and the criminology of place', Criminology, Vol.27, No.1, pp.27-55.

SHERMAN, L.W. and WEISBURD, D. (1992) Does Patrol Prevent Crime? The Minneapolis Hot Spots Experiment. Washington, D.C.: Crime Control Institute.

SHERNOCK, S.K. (1986) 'A Profile Of The Citizen Crime Prevention Activist' Journal of Criminal Justice., 14, 211-228.

SILBERMAN, C.E. (1978) Criminal Violence, Criminal Justice. New York: Random House.
SKOGAN, W. (1988) 'Disorder, crime and community decline'. In: HOPE, T. and SHAW, M. (eds) Communities and Crime Reduction London: HMSO.

SKOGAN, W.G. (1990) Disorder and Decline: Crime and the Spiral of Decay in American Neighbourhoods. New York: Free Press.

SKOGAN, W.G. and WYCOFF, M.A. (1986) 'Storefront Police Officers: The Houston Field Test'. In: D.P. Rosenbaum (1986) Community Crime Prevention: Does It Work? London: Sage.

SMITH, C.S., FARRANT, M.R. and MARCHANT, H.J. (1972) The Wincroft Youth Project: A social work programme in a slum area. London: Tavistock Publications.

SMITH, M. (1980) 'TV-linked entry-phone system to safeguard high-rise tenancies', Housing, Vol.16, pp.10-12.

SMITH, D. (1994) An Evaluation of Two Detached Youth Work Projects in Wolverhampton
Unpublished Report to the Home Office Research and Planning Unit. London: Home Office.

SMITH, L. and BURROWS, J. (1986) 'Nobbling the fraudsters: crime prevention through administrative change', The Howard Journal, Vol.25, No.1, pp.13-24.

SORRENTINO, A. (1959) 'The Chicago Area Project after 25 Years'. Federal Probation. June. pp.40-45.

SOUTHALL, D. and EKBLOM, P. (1985) 'Designing for Car Security: towards a crime-free car.' Crime Prevention Unit Paper No. 4. London: Home Office Crime Prevention Unit.

SPELMAN, W. (1993) 'Abandoned buildings: magnets for crime', Journal of Criminal Justice, Vol.21, pp.481-495.

STANDING CONFERENCE ON CRIME PREVENTION. (1986) Report of the Working Group on Residential Burglary. London: Home Office.

STEINMETZ, C.H.D. (1982) 'A first step towards victimological risk analysis: A conceptual model for the prevention of "petty" crime.' In: KUEHLHORN, E. and SVENNSON, B. (eds.) Crime prevention. Stockholm: The National Swedish Council for Crime Prevention, Report No.9.

STURMAN, A. (1980) 'Damage on buses: The effects of supervision.' In: Clarke, R.V.G. and Mayhew, P. (eds.). Designing out Crime. London: HMSO.

TAGGART, R. (1981) 'A fisherman's guide: an assessment of training and remediation strategies.' Kalamazoo, Michigan: W.E. Upjohn Institute for Employment Research.

TARLING, R. (1982) 'Unemployment and crime.' Research Bulletin No. 14, London: Home Office Research and Planning Unit.
TARLING, R. (1993) Analysing Offending: Data, Models and Interpretations. London: HMSO.

TAUB, R., TAYLOR, D.G. and DUNHAM, J.D. (1984) Paths of Neighbourhood Change. Chicago: University of Chicago Press.

THE TIMES, 15 March, 1994.

TIEN, J.M., O'DONNELL, V.R., BARNETT, A.K. and MIRCHANDANE, P.B. (1979) 'Street Lighting Projects.' National Evaluation Program, Phase I. US Department of Justice: Washington, DC: Government Printing Office.

TILLEY, N. (1993) The Prevention Crime Against Small Businesses: The Safer Cities Experience. Crime Prevention Unit Paper No.45. London: Home Office.

TITUS, R. (1984), 'Residential Burglary and the Community Response', in Clarke, R.V.G. and Hope, T. Coping with Burglary. Boston: Kluwer-Nijhoff.

TRICKETT, A., OSBORN, D.K., SEYMOUR, J. and PEASE, K. (1992) 'What is different about high crime areas?' British Journal of Criminology, Vol.32, pp.81-90.

TROJANOWICZ, R.C. (1986) 'Evaluating a Neighbourhood Foot Patrol Program' in Rosenbaum, D.P. (1986) Community Crime Prevention: Does It Work? London: Sage.

TUCK, M. (1987) 'Crime prevention: a shift in concept.' In: Graham, J. (ed) Research Bulletin: Special European Edition, Home Office Research and Planning Unit, No. 24. London: HMSO.

UTTING, D., BRIGHT, J., and HENRICSON, C. (1993) 'Crime and the Family'. Family Policy Studies Centre. Occasional Paper 16. London.

VAHLENKAMP, W. (1989) Kriminalitaetsvorbeugung auf kommunaler Ebene. Wiesbaden: Bundeskriminalamt.

VAN ANDEL, H. (1989) 'Crime prevention that works: The care of public transport in the Netherlands.' British Journal of Criminology, vol.29, no.1, pp 47-57.

VAN DIJK, J.J.M and STEINMETZ, C. (1981) An Evaluation of the National Publicity Campaigns. The Hague: Research and Documentation Centre, Ministry of Justice.

VAN DIJK, J.J., MAYHEW, P. and KILLIAS, M. (1991) Experiences of Crime Across the World: Key findings from the 1989 International crime Survey. Deventer: Kluwer.

VAN DIJK, J. and DE WAARD, J. (1991) ' A two-dimensional typology of crime prevention projects: with a bibliography', Criminal Justice Abstracts, Vol.23, pp.483-503.

VAN VOORHIS, P. (1986) 'Delinquency prevention: Towards comprehensive models and a conceptual map.' Criminal Justice Review, vol.11, no.1, pp 15-24. WALKER, S., WALKER, C. and McDAVID, J. (1992) The Victoria Community Police Stations: A Three Year Evaluation. Ottawa: Canadian Police College.

WALLER, I. (1991) Introductory Report: Putting Crime Prevention on the Map Paris: Proceedings of an International Conference on Urban Safety, Drugs and Crime Prevention.

WALMSLEY, R. HOWARD, L. and WHITE, S. (1991). 'The National Prison Survey 1991: Main Findings'. Home Office Research Study No. 128. London: HMSO.

WEBB, B. (1994) 'Steering Column Locks and Motor vehicle Theft: Evaluations from three countries'; In: R. V. Clarke (ed.) Crime Prevention Studies Volume 2: Monsey, NY: Criminal Justice Press.

WEST, D.J. (1982) Delinquency: Its Roots, Careers and Prospects. London: Heinemann.
WILES, P. (1992) 'Ghettoization in Europe?' European Journal on Criminal Policy and Research. Vol.1, pp.52-69.

WILSON, J.Q. and KELLING, G.L. (1982) 'Broken windows: the police and neighbourhood safety'. The Atlantic Monthly, (March) pp 29-38.

WILSON, H. (1980) 'Parental Supervision: a neglected aspect of delinquency'. British Journal of Criminology, vol. 20, no. 3, pp 203-235.

WILSON, H. (1987) 'Parental Supervision Re-examined'. British Journal of Criminology, vol. 27, no. 3, pp 275-301.

WILSON, S (1980) 'Vandalism and defensible space on London housing estates' In: R. V. G Clarke and P. Mayhew Designing out crime. London: HMSO.

WRIGHT, J.D., ROSSI, P.H. and DALY, K. (1983) Under the Gun: Weapons, crime and violence in America. New York: Aldine.

WRIGHT, R. and DECKER, S. (1994) Burglars on the Job. Boston: Northeastern University Press.

WYCOFF, M.A. and SKOGAN, W. (1993) 'Community policing in Madison: an analysis of implementation and impact'. In: D. Rosenbaum. The Challenge of Community Policing: Testing the Promises. London: Sage.

YIN, R.K., VOGEL, M.E., CHAIKEN, J.M. and BOTH, D.R. (1977) Citizen Patrol Projects. U.S. Department of Justice. Washington, D.C.: Government Printing Office.

YOSHIKAWA, H. (1993) 'Prevention as Cumulative Protection: Effects of Early Family Support and Education on Chronic Delinquency and Its Risks'. Psychological Bulletin. vol. 115, no.1, pp. 1-27.

ZIGLER, E. and HALL, N.W. (1987) 'The implications of early intervention efforts for the primary prevention of juvenile delinquency.' In Wilson, J.Q. and Loury, G.C. (eds.) Families, schools and delinquency prevention, vol. III of 'From Children to Citizens'. New York: Springer Verlag.

ZIMBARDO, P.G. (1973) 'A field experiment in auto-shaping'. In: C. Ward (ed.) Vandalism. London: Architectural Press.